THE ALL-YEAR-ROUND
CHRISTMAS HANDBOOK

THE ALL-YEAR-ROUND
CHRISTMAS HANDBOOK

PLAN, MAKE, COOK, AND CREATE YOUR OWN UNIQUE CELEBRATION

WRITTEN AND ILLUSTRATED BY TIFFANY WOOD

CICO BOOKS
LONDON NEW YORK

DEDICATION

An infectious delight in celebrating Christmas well is the treasured legacy of my Grandma, Audrey Gwendoline Davis, née Adams (1919–1992). Loved beyond words by her very large family and special friends, her house was always full to the brim with Christmas cards, carefully counted and displayed with enormous pride. Christmas meals were heavenly chaos, when piano stools and ironing boards were drafted in as makeshift seats, party hats and silly games were obligatory, and eating and laughing too much were the treasured order of Christmas Day. As her beloved son Andrew so rightly says to me, "Grandma's Christmases still play out every year all over the place," and nowhere more so than in this book. Each year, may my children, Holly, Rosa, and George be filled with that same Christmas joy, their whole lives long.

Published in 2020 by CICO Books
An imprint of Ryland Peters & Small Ltd
20–21 Jockey's Fields, London WC1R 4BW
341 E 116th St, New York, NY 10029

www.rylandpeters.com

10 9 8 7 6 5 4 3 2 1

Text and illustrations © Tiffany Wood 2020
Design © CICO Books 2020

A CIP catalog record for this book is available from the Library of Congress and the British Library.

ISBN: 978 1 78249 891 9

Printed in China

Art director: Sally Powell
Production controller: David Hearn
Head of production: Patricia Harrington
Publishing manager: Penny Craig
Publisher: Cindy Richards

NOTE: Both American (imperial and US cups) and British (metric) measurements are included in the recipes for your convenience. However, it is important to work with only one set of measurements and not alternate between the two within a recipe.

INTRODUCTION

"Let's make Christmas our pause button, when we
mindfully cherish special people around us and
find fleeting moments of true contentment."

BEING MRS CHRISTMAS

Bear your name with pride if you have taken on the role of Mrs Christmas in your house, and please accept my apology for adopting the feminine form here for the sake of convenience; I most certainly mean any enthusiastic soul of any gender who revels in the glory of Christmas preparation! I like to think we are joy-generating powerhouses of celebration. Our capacity to care about marking the season well enhances the lives of our loved ones, year in, year out. My own Christmas is a very English one, but how lucky we are, all around the world, to follow on from countless generations of Mrs Christmases before us, who have passed on their different ways of celebrating Christmas which endure to this day.

But stop right there, some may say—how does Father Christmas (or Santa Claus) fit in then, if it's Mrs C who's really the festive mover and shaker? Is he redundant or—dare they ask—did he ever really exist? My answer is this: let's say he doesn't look after all things Christmassy with quite her efficiency and he's not that easy to find in the North Pole, but he truly is in every home where Mrs Christmas and her loved ones keep the spirit of Christmas alive.

Father Christmas personifies kindness and love for little ones, with a spectacular dollop of festive magic. Along with many other Mrs Christmases, I am still enraptured by his shimmering spell, carrying out my Christmas preparations in the shadow of dear and cherished memories of him. We Mrs Christmases appreciate just how real Father Christmas still is, because he's part of our purposeful plans as we scribble and sort, review and refine—and he's at the very heart of our sentimental selves.

CHRISTMAS TRADITIONS

My festive memories of growing up as one of four sisters in West Germany in the 1970s have undoubtedly shaped my Christmas tastes and pleasures. To this day, visiting Germany one crisp, cold weekend each December is a delicious transportation back in time for me, to the heady levels of festive joy that perhaps we feel only as children. Potent emotions are entangled in the season, resurrected on the strain of a favorite carol or the waft of a warm mince pie (see page 104); or in the case of one lady in the 1930s, the fondly remembered smell of tiny candles burning on her family's Christmas tree when she was a child in the late Victorian era. As an adult, one of her greatest sadnesses was that colored electric "globes" had replaced the wobbly colored candles she'd loved so much.

With an unusually fond regard for the way our parents did things, we decorate our homes, we make merry, and sometimes worship. We hang up stockings or put out shoes, light candles and open advent calendars, bring evergreens indoors, and bake our national specialities full of spices. We sing carols we know by heart and stuff ourselves with festive food (even if we don't much like some of it!). They are rituals we've learned, all firmly rooted in the past. Nostalgic forces of goodwill are mightily powerful at this time of year, no better illustrated than in the Christmas truces on the battlefields of World War One in 1914.

Charles Dickens well understood the power of festive sentimentality when he penned *A Christmas Carol* back in 1843. Scrooge's lesson in "how to keep Christmas well" was taken to heart by his adoring audience. They delighted too in ancient customs from Germany, like the Christmas tree, made popular by Queen Victoria and her consort Prince Albert. Around this time, Father Christmas, once just a figure of good cheer with a holly wreath atop his bearded head, morphed into a chubby, red-robed, and thoroughly "old-fashioned" giver of presents to children. How delightful it is that whenever and wherever we live, festive ways embraced by our ancestors still zing with joyous life.

A SIMPLER CHRISTMAS

The Scandinavian concept of *hygge* draws upon our natural affinity with what's traditional and familiar—a contentment and sense of sanctuary, when we feel comfortable, safe, and protected from anything unpredictable or unpleasant. *Hygge* takes the focus away from individuals, their status or achievements, and instead puts it on relationships, community, and living simply, whether we are snuggling under a blanket with a good book and a hot water bottle, cozying up in candlelight, or enjoying hearty food with friends and family.

A *hyggelig* Christmas takes concerted thought and effort today, when levels of festive consumption, commercialism, and social isolation are so shamefully high. You may well feel huge cynicism about Christmas as a result, just like a dear friend I'll call Mrs Humbug Christmas. She tells me that for her, Christmas looms like Everest, as the dreaded countdown starts earlier each year, with TV commercials and social media posts depicting homely harmony in snowy wonderlands, lavish festive feasts, and piles of polluting, profligate presents that give us nothing but the briefest thrill. She turns her back on the whole thing.

To you, my dear cold-footed friend, I say that Christmas need not be like that. Celebrated more simply, more thoughtfully and in a more homespun way, it really is worth the effort. Not everyone needs or wants to reach the Christmas pinnacle, but we can all find a version of Christmas that appeals uniquely to us.

How do we create a more mindful Christmas? We can start by abandoning all hope of perfection; dealing with the tricky, sad, unexpected, and even disastrous, is a very real part of the task. If we think back to the most special Christmases we have ever had, it won't ever be the detail that clinched it. The true challenge of organizing Christmas is knowing what really matters, and slowing down so that *hygge* doesn't pass us by.

In our super speedy lives, let's make Christmas our pause button, when we mindfully cherish special people around us and find fleeting moments of true contentment.

HOW TO USE THIS BOOK

Christmas is a time to count and celebrate our blessings, as we gather together all the things we treasure most in life—for me that's family, dearest friends, the heavenly winter comforts of kitchen and hearth, and the chance to be creative. Every year, I set myself the challenge of being as well organized as possible in advance, with the busiest bits in the bag by early December, so I can then properly savor the season. I can't help wanting to dabble in lots of activities, so what works for me is thorough planning, starting in plenty of time, and keeping everything I do extra easy in the winter months. I do indulge in all sorts of things that are not strictly essential, simply because of the creativity they involve, but if I want to tackle a project that takes more than a few hours, I don't leave it until the run-up to Christmas.

I have taken the calendar as the basis for this book, and woven my own Christmassy tasks into it. I am aware of festive preparations throughout the year—albeit very faintly from February through to October—and without in any way compromising the enjoyment of each season, or the renewed delight as Christmas approaches. All year round I keep an ear or an eye out for inspired suggestions, whether a gift, a handmade project, a recipe, or a different approach. Alongside my own strategies I set out those of the most organized and creative Mrs and Mr Christmases I know. Skip what makes you feel queasy—which for my three sisters probably means most of it, as they merely laugh when they see my timetables! For them, I introduce a few ideas from Mrs Nimble Christmas, a devoted disciple of The Simple and The Shortcut, who has no patience for anything requiring too much skill or time.

There are no prescriptions here. To my mind, there's no one way, no ultimate manual, and no place for fashion when it comes to Christmas. Sentimentality permits tastes as vulgar as we please, family habits as mad as they come. I chart my annual journey merely to inspire any Mrs Christmas who might like to create his or her own logistical blueprint, which can be developed for reference through the years. The blank planning pages in each chapter, for you to fill in yourself, are the most important ones by far.

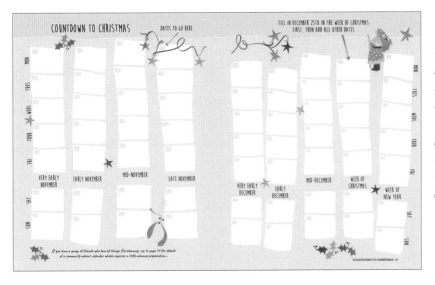

The Countdown to Christmas calendar on pages 20–21 provides an overview of the run-up to the festivities. I've given each week a name, and these form the basis for many of the chapters which follow. Don't forget to fill in December 25th in the week of Christmas first, then work backward and forward filling in the other dates.

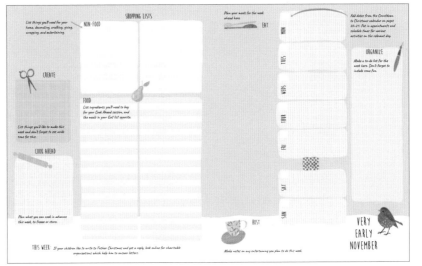

On pages 34–35 and then in each chapter, you'll find a blank double-page planning dashboard for that particular week. Fill in the dates to match those in the Countdown to Christmas calendar. These pages provide space to organize and chart every aspect of your Christmas preparations.

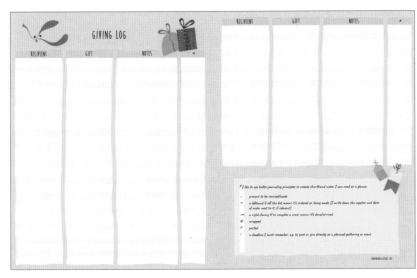

Dotted throughout the book are other organizer pages for you to fill in. If you need replacement pages for future years, or you'd rather work on loose pages that you can file away for reference, then visit www.rylandpeters.com, where these pages can be downloaded for printing at home.

CHAPTER 1

325 DAYS TO CHRISTMAS

"Christmas would lose its shine if it lingered beyond January—but that's not to say a wise Mrs Christmas doesn't keep alert to the odd prop or plan which might come in handy next time."

ALL YEAR ROUND

Christmas would lose its shine if it lingered beyond early January. But that's not to say a wise Mrs Christmas doesn't stay alert all year to the odd prop or plan which might come in handy next time round. After the shopping splurges of November, December, and the January sales, I usually find I have a few smart paper carrier bags and pleasing packaging which is too lovely and too extravagant to dump in the recycling bin. Far better I store the best of them for adapting or embellishing next Christmas, so one of our suitcases gets drafted in for the job.

There's other packaging to keep from the seasonal indulgences in the kitchen too; scrubbed aluminum foil trays will be handy for freezing and cooking meals during the year, as well as next Christmas. I like to squirrel away colorful tea, cookie, and cereal boxes, beautifully shaped jars and bottles, shallow clear plastic punnets (the type used for soft fruit), and the small wooden boxes in which soft cheeses are packaged.

From January, Mrs NK Christmas saves money every month toward the following Christmas—just like the readers of *Wife and Home* magazine back in 1935, who were told to spread party spirit and smiles everywhere at Christmas—which was more manageable by those who saved a regular sum all year round and cut their Yuletide garment to suit their cloth.

Pretty much all I manage to save are the fruits of a few good springtime yard or jumble sales. I am in my element whiling away happy hours in search of treasure—items with old buttons and buckles, paste jewelry (broken is fine), vintage bowls, tins, or baskets, and old books with lovely illustrations. If I'm lucky I'll find some nice linen or, on a very good day, some hole-ridden cashmere for my craft box. Interesting or pleasing fabric (whether for its print, texture, or color), even in the form of a thoroughly undesirable garment, is worth collecting too—at the very least for learning how to wrap gifts with fabric the Japanese way, known as *furoshiki*, which I am currently trying to master.

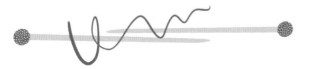

MAKING AHEAD

Once I have my materials, I start pondering what I might make this year. I may tackle at least one bigger project, with Christmas at the back of my mind, either for our own home or to give as an extra-special present next year. Any specifically festive detail can be added later, but I get the basic bits nailed early. Over the years I have made fairies for the top and skirts for the bottom of Christmas trees, table-runners and sets of napkins, stockings and sacks, fabric wreaths and advent calendars, strings of white cashmere pom-poms (from one of those sweaters I unraveled), and garlands of felted shapes glued to curly paper-covered wire. These projects sometimes take more than a single year to complete, but luckily Christmas always comes round again.

All year long, I stealthily add to my hoard of crafting materials—I peel ribbons and bits of smart wrapping paper very carefully from presents I'm given, and save pleasing envelopes and paper bags. Then one rainy day (or two, here in Britain) I can get out my sewing machine and make myself a big pile of simple paper gift bags, in all shapes and sizes.

Using these bags to present gifts is both a handy and planet-friendly way to go, not just for Christmas but for birthdays and any other occasion. They are great for holding awkwardly-shaped presents, or tiny ones you'd like to disguise—and best of all they're speedy, without the need for scissors and sticky tape. And of course if they're sturdy enough, they can be used several times over. Creating bags using a sewing machine was an idea inspired by a lovely old potato sack I once had. They're great fun and just need a little practice to get the feel of working on paper or thin card, though the same concept would work equally well with fabric, especially for heavier items, such as bottles.

SNAZZY BAGS AND POSH POTATO SACKS

For the snazzy bags, with your sewing machine on its longest stitch setting and using a sturdy needle, simply sew two flattened thicknesses of a cheerful paper carrier bag together in any shape you like, then cut off the excess a little outside of your stitch line. Replace the handles if you fancy and add a festive embellishment and label to finish. Pop your gift inside and stuff in a little tissue paper or some shreds of recycled wrap to conceal it.

For the potato sack design, take one strong bag or envelope and trim off the top with pinking shears or fancy scissors.

Cut a 2in (5cm) strip of contrasting wrap slightly longer than the width of the bag and fold it in half, then slot it over the base. Machine-sew in running stitch with ends left loose.

To close the potato sack, fold over the top, and seal with a sticky label, or wind twine around top to bottom, or punch in a pair of holes to weave through some ribbon or raffia, with an embellishment if you like.

SPRING AND SUMMER

Once the spring sunshine beckons, my thoughts turn away from crafting and out to the garden, where I might plant some bulbs or winter-flowering plants, and tend anything there that will be perfect for cutting, drying, and using at Christmas time. My favorites are poppy heads and hydrangeas—those lime green and ruby red ones in particular—which I cut at the end of summer, when their color is still strong and before they begin to brown, ideally with a good stem on them and just above any new buds. I strip the leaves off and place them in a vase half full of water, out of direct sunlight, then I leave them for a few weeks without topping up the water to let them dry out gently. Poppy heads can just hang upside down in the shed or porch to dry.

When traveling in the summer, I may buy the odd item that will make a lovely present—beautiful local specialties which are more easily sourced abroad, such as olive wood platters from Greece, or leather or stationery from Italy. If we are in France, then stocking up on a few favorite food items (especially soft cheese for the freezer and, of course, some wine!) is a must too. Mrs SR Christmas buys a decoration for her Christmas tree from every faraway land she visits. I always aim to find some exquisitely wrapped candies from wherever I go on holiday, which I eventually pass on to Santa with toes of stockings in mind. I also like to buy a foreign newspaper or two to add to my wrapping stash.

Whenever I remember in the second half of the year, I book theatre, ballet, or pantomime tickets for the Christmas season ahead—it seems a very long way off, but it's sobering if you stop to count the days. Where has this year gone, I ask myself, again. The sense of the fleeting year for me is most marked in the hazy fading of late summer, in the flurry of buying school shoes and new pencil cases. Before long, for those of us in colder climes, our feet are swishing through fallen leaves, wood smoke's in the air, and we are back seeking refuge indoors—our nests taking center stage again. I treasure this seasonal shift and the renewed homage we pay to all that is cozy, as fall sets in.

There are plenty of garden plants that look wonderful cut and displayed in a vase. Cyclamen coum or Helleborus niger (the Christmas rose) and even greenery like holly, mistletoe, and Scots pine will all last far longer when kept in water.

Honesty

Bash the stems of hellebore so they can fully absorb the water.

Hydrangeas

Long stems of berries in vases, with other greenery like holly, make bold colorful displays which require no skill and minimal time. Dog roses with hips can be foraged or, if your climate is suitable, grow wild roses in your garden—they produce fat, vivid, orangey-red hips.

Winter berry

At the end of the summer, harvest any plants which look beautiful in their dried state and make marvelous additions to your festive display, or tie them on to presents for a natural decoration. Dried alliums or agapanthus heads (and poppies too) look very glitzy when sprayed with metallic paint or given the glue and (biodegradable) glitter treatment!

Rosa Rigosa (wild rose)

Snowberry

Poppies

Rosemary is a very useful plant to have in your garden, for both cooking and decorating. I love to have some dark green glossy holly growing in my garden, and some ivy on the walls, though both can be foraged from the wild! Christmas box (Sarcococca confusa) makes pretty little arrangements in vases, with its dark green leaves and clusters of tiny white flowers.

CHAPTER 2

SEPTEMBER AND OCTOBER

"Before we head into the depths of winter ... there are a few tasks which, when done early, will smooth the festive path."

PLANNING AHEAD

September and October are months loaded with anticipation—of gathering supplies and preparing for the coming weeks before we head into the depths of winter. But until Halloween is well out of the way, I turn a grumpy blind eye to all things Christmassy in the shops. At the same time, I recognize there are a few tasks which, when done early, will smooth the festive path. My first happy task is to make a Countdown to Christmas planner, for a detailed overview of the calendar. I mark it up with birthdays, concerts and services, school plays and shows, work parties and other events—and the boring but essential stuff, like last posting dates and revised refuse collections. Next I'll write in any Christmas workshops or courses (which are treats to be researched as early as possible) and festive fairs too. Some of these take place soon, which means being organized early to liaise with friends, buy tickets, and plan.

Now's the time to think about anything on a long lead time that you want to get sorted before Christmas, whether that's buying new furniture or booking in some professional help (I always seems to realize a room needs decorating as I contemplate the arrival of multiple guests), the service of an appliance, or the cleaning of the oven or the carpets. If you plan to hold a big party, deciding on caterers and any other essentials early means you've got a better chance of securing exactly what you want, especially if you choose a popular date close to Christmas.

Mrs CS Christmas buys hyacinth and paper white narcissus bulbs now, so they can be planted up and stored in the shed for their dark and cool phase, prior to early December when they come indoors to the warmth and light. They make perfect offerings at Christmas time, especially if you can find some lovely pots or vintage bowls to plant them in.

COUNTDOWN TO CHRISTMAS

DATES TO GO HERE

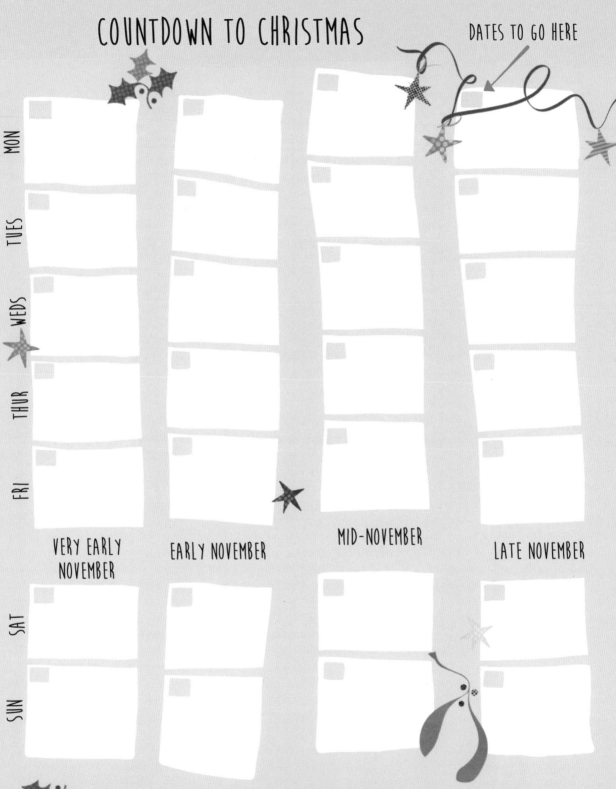

MON

TUES

WEDS

THUR

FRI

VERY EARLY
NOVEMBER

EARLY NOVEMBER

MID-NOVEMBER

LATE NOVEMBER

SAT

SUN

*If you have a group of friends who love all things Christmassy, nip to page 79 for details
of a community advent calendar which requires a little advance preparation...*

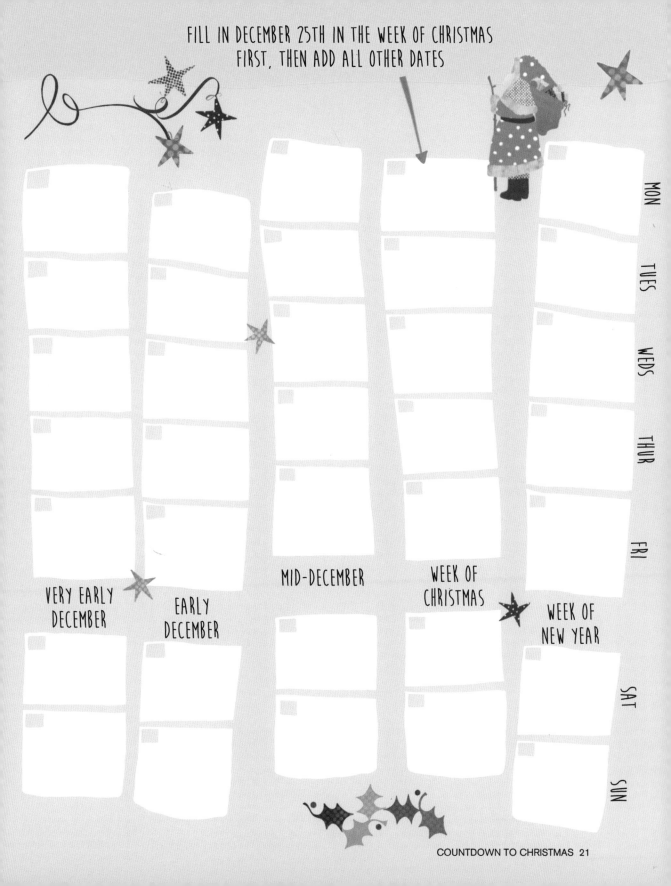

FILL IN DECEMBER 25TH IN THE WEEK OF CHRISTMAS
FIRST, THEN ADD ALL OTHER DATES

MON

TUES

WEDS

THUR

FRI

VERY EARLY
DECEMBER

EARLY
DECEMBER

MID-DECEMBER

WEEK OF
CHRISTMAS

WEEK OF
NEW YEAR

SAT

SUN

HARVEST TIME

In the kitchen, now is the ideal time for gardeners with produce to make jams and chutneys—or great quantities of applesauce for freezing in our case! That prompts me to start organizing my freezer and noting exactly what's been in there long enough, so we can eat it up over the coming weeks. I go through the larder in the same way, sorting through out-of-date items and taking stock. At some point in October, the big supermarket chains release their Christmas grocery delivery slots, so I get in there early and reserve the times I'm most likely to want.

Out on walks I seek out fallen acorns and pine cones. Blackberry picking is a must, too—for jam and blackberry liqueur, to make and give away. I also keep an eye out for the ripening of damsons or sloes for foraging at the perfect moment, to add to gin. Once these alcoholic infusions (which are so simple to make) have had a few months to mellow, they can be decanted into glass bottles which have been squirreled away during the year, then decorated and labeled for timely Christmas sharing.

TIP
EARLY FALL IS THE PERFECT TIME FOR A BIG CLEAR OUT OF TOYS, BOOKS, CLOTHING, HOMEWARE, AND SO ON, TO TAKE TO CHARITY STORES. I JUST KEEP BACK THE ODD FEW THINGS THAT MIGHT BE PERFECT TO DONATE TO SCHOOL OR CHURCH FOR A FUNDRAISING STALL OR RAFFLE PRIZE.

FRUITY BOOZE

USE GOOD QUALITY ALCOHOL HERE—DON'T LET CHEAP STUFF SPOIL YOUR TOIL!

DAMSON GIN
SENSATIONAL SERVED ON ICE

Freeze 1lb/500g of clean and de-stalked damsons overnight in a freezer bag, then still in the bag, bash them gently (a rolling pin works well). Place the damsons in a 4¼-pt/2-liter lidded jar with 4 cups/1 liter of gin and 1½ cups/275g superfine (caster) sugar. Shake the jar every day for a week, fully dissolving the sugar, then leave it in a cool dark place until December. Strain and decant into clean, dry bottles.

STORAGE AND PRESENTATION

Collect glass fruit juice and sauce bottles during the year (I always look for unusual ones when I'm abroad). Wrap the lid in a disc of paper and finish with a label, or write on the glass with a white paint pen. Store the bottles in a cool, dark place.

BLACKBERRY LIQUEUR
A TEASPOON OR TWO OF THIS IN A GLASS OF CHAMPAGNE MAKES A DELICIOUS COCKTAIL.

In a 4¼-pt/2-liter lidded jar, roughly squash 4 cups/600g blackberries (a potato masher works well) and then cover with a bottle of red wine. Leave for a few days to infuse, then sieve into a saucepan. Add 3 cups/600g sugar and simmer for 5 minutes. Cool, stir in 1 cup/250ml brandy or vodka, then decant into clean, dry bottles.

CHAPTER 3

VERY EARLY NOVEMBER

"It is a truth which it has taken me a lot of Christmases to realize, that an organized November makes way for a serene December."

EARLY TO RISE

It is a truth which has taken me lots of Christmases to realize, that an organized November makes way for a serene December. I should probably admit here that from now on, I get up half an hour earlier on weekday mornings (definitely not the weekends, since snuggly lie-ins are the happy upside to cold, dark mornings).

I know the very idea sounds punishing, but try it for a week and abandon if it doesn't help you! I get into a treasured routine that creates quiet time for me to plan and reflect. I light some candles, put on music quietly and, with a mug of tea, thoroughly enjoy the tranquility. My sense of contentment reminds me—no doubt looking through rose-tinted spectacles—of those half-awake hours with my newborn babies in the middle of the night, while the rest of the world was asleep. The few extra hours in the week that this gives me really do make a difference, but Mrs Nimble Christmas will probably do no such thing; she prides herself on cutting back Christmas preparations to the most glorious essentials only, aiming for maximum effect with minimum stress.

THE JOY OF GIVING

Now is the time to go through my present stash—things I've gathered ready for any occasion, not just Christmas. During the year, I might have made a few gifts, or bought some in the sales, so I can give generously without breaking the budget. All year I'm mindful of directing Father Christmas in his stocking-filling duties, so I keep an eye out for smaller gifts which might be of use to him. Spreading the buying out through the year helps with budgeting too. I keep notes of what I've collected and put gifts straight into a chest I keep especially for this purpose—otherwise I've been known to forget, double buy, or not be able to find that specific present just when I need it. I can hear Mrs Humbug Christmas tutting at me now—and rightly so. But perhaps this is the moment to reassure her that a gradual gathering and careful consideration of each little gift (which does not have to be expensive, merely pleasing) can be a pleasure, not a chore.

About now, I turn my head and pencil to drawing up my Christmas Giving Log (see pages 30–31)—a list of every person I plan to give a present to.

A NOTE FROM MRS NIMBLE

- Start preparations early and spread them out evenly in the run-up to Christmas.

- Think about which preparations give you pleasure and which can be delegated or dropped.

- Write yourself two big lists, one of everything you'd like to buy and another of everything you'd like to do. Keep them flexible and add or subtract as you fancy.

- Give fewer presents with just one or two themes or suppliers for everyone; perhaps experiences or ethical gifts that fit into envelopes to avoid parcel-posting queues.

- Use your time efficiently on the internet for both your present and food shopping. Local independent shopping is loveliest of all, but if time is short, save that for special sourcing.

- Keep everything in the kitchen simple, using fewer but high-quality items, or try companies that have grouped together the ingredients for you. Take advantage of good-quality ready-made products which save time and stress.

- Keep plenty of space in the diary for downtime and relaxation, avoiding too many commitments.

- If you'd like to entertain friends, consider doing so one day after Christmas, when everyone (and your home) is still in celebratory mode, but things are a little more relaxed.

- Look out for nimble recipes, and time- and stress-saving strategies dotted throughout this book. Very few Christmas preparations are essential, so prioritize pleasure instead!

PRESENT STASH

I keep my gifts in a lockable chest made for me by my father, but a suitcase would do just as well.

I gather presents to put inside whenever I come across an ideal gift. My hoard may also include the odd special item I've been given which I already have or is unsuitable.

CAUTION

Gift recycling requires either honesty or very great care. Never pass on the mediocre—receiving something we suspect is a reject is grim!

HELPING FATHER CHRISTMAS

Inside the chest, I keep individual bags for every person receiving multiple presents. As gifts are added to these, a Father Christmas gift-list (see pages 28–29) comes in handy to keep track of them.

I use a box file to keep all my receipts in.

FATHER CHRISTMAS GIFT LISTS

NAME:

IDEAS AND WISHES

NAME:

IDEAS AND WISHES

GIVING LOG

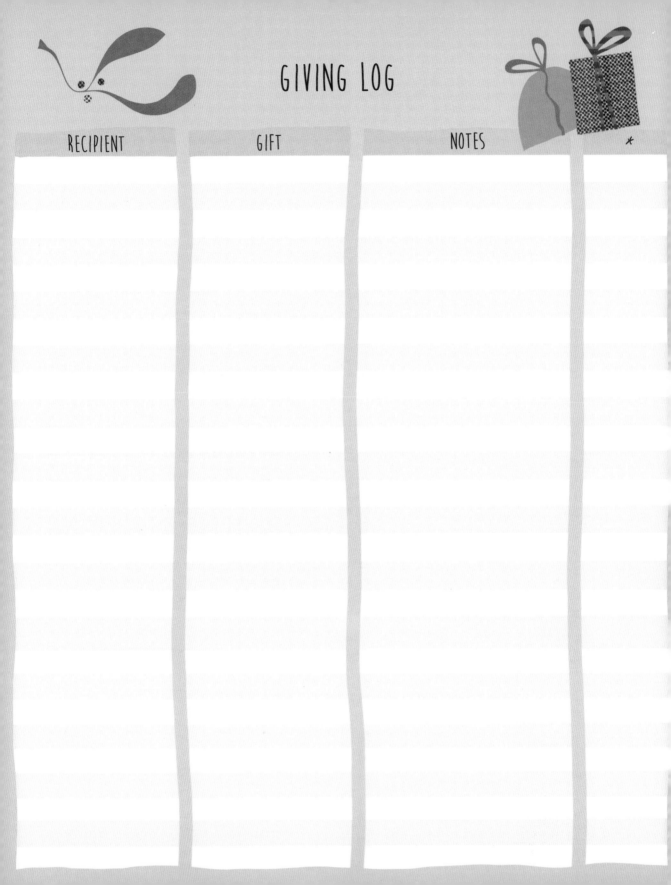

RECIPIENT	GIFT	NOTES	✗

RECIPIENT	GIFT	NOTES	*

*I like to use bullet-journaling principles to create shorthand notes I can read at a glance:

- •   present to be sourced/made
- >•   a lefthand V off the dot means it's ordered or being made (I write down the supplier and date of order next to it, if relevant)
- ✕   a right-facing V to complete a cross means it's done/arrived
- W   wrapped
- P   posted
- !   a deadline I must remember, e.g. to post or give directly at a planned gathering or event

PLANET-FRIENDLY GIVING

Will they absolutely love it, or does it meet a true need?

Are the materials and packaging natural or recycled? (or look for pre-loved plastic toys!)

Am I supporting local trade and artisans?

How best can I buy a present? Always ask yourself...

Is the quality good and long lasting?

Could something precious I own make a special gift (perhaps an heirloom to the younger generation?)

Can I give a promise or intent?

For example, a homemade voucher to polish some shoes—to plant summer bulbs—to babysit—to make a meal or breakfast in bed—to wash the car—to give technical help or the promise of a weekly video call (both great for grandparents!)

For family or groups of friends, how about a "secret Santa" plan?

Could we adopt a "child only" rule to reduce the number of gifts exchanged?

Could I give something intangible, or an experience?

Could I give an ethical or charitable present, either in developing countries or closer to home?

Might I give a group or family present instead of separate ones?

Such as a day trip or weekend away —a subscription or membership— a masterclass in wine tasting, car mechanics, make-up, bread making or craft—a ticket or a special meal

Could I give a homemade present?

Such as tickets to the cinema or ice rink—a board game—a hammock—a kite—a bird-feeder

GIVING WELL

I'm always listening out for present ideas, so there's less need to request written wish lists which can feel too materialistic and lack the element of surprise. Doing a little homework helps too. Mrs JM Christmas quietly asks parents, partners, friends, or siblings of the recipient for advice on presents that will be just right.

Let's not take inspiration from the pages of 1950s and '60s women's magazines which were stuffed with suggestions they thought genius—lipstick for ladies, whose lips should be luscious, provocative, soft, and inviting; a silver-plated butter curler or some Pyrex ovenware for girlfriends; a handkerchief gift set for fathers; a wooden cigarette box for husbands; or, even better, a "manly" gift of an electric powered drill. Give a beloved wife a Hoover (advised Hoover Ltd), something that will add joy to her new year.

If ever our own imagination is so lacking that we feel a household appliance coming on, perhaps we should remind ourselves of gifts we've received, which were plain impersonal, dull, or worse. And bearing in mind the impact of consumerism on our planet, might we give more intangible offerings that bring us together, rather than pressing on with gifts which will only add to our clutter, which Mrs Humbug Christmas rightly cannot bear? Recycling is integral to a responsible approach to Christmas, but the key is a simple reduction in what we consume in the first place—of shopping, wrapping, posting, wasting, and polluting.

PLANNING WELL

As different elements of Christmas preparation loom, I draw up large-format planners, one for each week up to Christmas, covering every aspect in one dashboard layout. Seeing the weeks set out to include all my to-do and shopping lists, rather than using my normal diary, clears my head and aids my memory.

The day-by-day sections enable me to block out specific time for either one project or similar tasks I can batch together. When it comes to creativity, I set a time for a specific activity—say cooking, crafting, or wrapping—though precisely which I choose to do on the day can still be a spontaneous affair. From here on, these weekly planners will appear at the end of each chapter.

SHOPPING LISTS

List things you'll need for your home, decorating, crafting, giving, wrapping, and entertaining.

NON-FOOD

FOOD

List ingredients you'll need to buy for your Cook Ahead session, and the meals in your Eat list opposite.

CREATE

List things you'd like to make this week and don't forget to set aside time for this.

COOK AHEAD

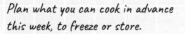

Plan what you can cook in advance this week, to freeze or store.

THIS WEEK: *If your children like to write to Father Christmas and get a reply, look online for charitable organizations which help him to answer letters.*

Plan your meals for the week ahead here.

EAT

MON

TUES

WEDS

THUR

FRI

SAT

SUN

HOST

Add dates from the Countdown to Christmas calendar on pages 20–21. Put in appointments and schedule times for various activities on the relevant day.

ORGANIZE

Make a to-do list for the week here. Don't forget to include some fun.

VERY
EARLY
NOVEMBER

Make notes on any entertaining you plan to do this week.

COOKING AHEAD

My "cook ahead" sessions on the planning dashboards are for Christmas food which can be made in advance, and stored in the larder or freezer. For each of the next eight weeks I suggest a few recipes you can make in the same session, to be more energy-efficient in terms of your own time management and in making best use of the already-heated oven. It means several culinary boxes can be ticked at the same time, with just one messy kitchen to tackle afterwards. And if I'm organized enough to have just one comprehensive shopping list covering cook-ahead preparation as well as day-to-day meals, then food shopping can be far less time-consuming too.

For highly organized Mr JW Christmas, the first big session in his kitchen takes place around now, when he makes his mincemeat and, most importantly, the Christmas cake, so it can be fed regularly with brandy for the next couple of months. I tend to delay all that soaking and stirring of fragrant festive ingredients a bit longer and instead kick off by making a few jars of relish or preserve, which also need time for their flavors to mature. They are extraordinarily simple—no skill required at all—yet a single session in the kitchen, using just one pan for each recipe (and electronic scales that can be set to zero each time you add a new ingredient), gives us jars of deliciousness which add zest to leftovers, snacks, and mealtimes throughout the holidays and can also be given away as gifts for those hard-to-buy-for people who already have everything.

In truth, I rarely manage to cook ahead every week in the run-up to Christmas, but anything I do make in advance feels like a godsend in the midst of the final flurry of busy Christmas preparations.

EACH RECIPE WILL MAKE 2-3 JARS
Clean dry jars can be sterilized by placing in
an oven at 350°F/gas mark 4/180°C for
5 minutes—fill when still warm.

CARAMELIZED RED ONION CHUTNEY

Heat 5tbsp/90ml olive oil and 5tbsp/75g butter in a large pan, then add 6 finely-sliced large red onions and ¾ cup/150g sugar. Cook over medium heat for 15–20 minutes then stir in ⅔ cup/175ml balsamic vinegar and 2½ cups/600ml dry red wine with a few peppercorns, 2 bay leaves, and 1tsp sea salt. Bring to a boil, simmer for 30–40 minutes until reduced to a jam-like consistency, then pour into sterilized jars and seal.

PRESERVES AND RELISHES

BOOZY PRUNES IN PORT

Place in a big pan the peeled zest and juice of a large unwaxed orange, 1 cup/200g sugar, 4 cups/600g dried and stoned prunes, a large pinch of ground ginger, and 3 cups/750ml water. Simmer very gently for an hour (without the lid on) then remove from heat and stir in ¾ cup/200ml port or Armagnac. When cool, pour into sterilized jars and seal.

I ALWAYS MAKE A LARGE JAR OF THESE—THEY TASTE HEAVENLY WITH ICE CREAM, GET EVEN BETTER WITH AGE, AND ARE A GREAT STANDBY TO HAVE ON HAND FOR A QUICK, BUT IMPRESSIVE, DESSERT.

FABULOUS FIG RELISH

YOU MAY PREFER TO MAKE YOUR MINCEMEAT THIS WEEK! (MY RECIPE IS ON PAGE 156.)

Finely chop 3 cups/450g dried figs, 1 peeled and cored apple, 1 large onion, and 4 pieces of stem ginger. Place them all in a big saucepan along with ½ cup/100g light brown soft sugar, ½ cup/75g sultanas, ¾ cup/175ml red wine vinegar, 1½tsp sea salt, and 1tbsp/15ml stem ginger syrup. Stir and simmer very gently for an hour (without the lid on) to a jam-like consistency, adding water as necessary to prevent sticking. Pour it into sterilized jars and seal.

CHAPTER 4

EARLY NOVEMBER

"Every year it's my intention to celebrate in a more personal way—making more and shopping less..."

THE SOCIAL WHIRL

Questions about Christmas arrangements start to bubble up around now, so a family brainstorm might help get it into shape. Who's coming? What did we love last year? What might we do/eat/arrange? It's easy to get into a fixed social rut at Christmas time—on the whole, it's the familiar we love most. But this time of year gives us a great opportunity to bond with friends we don't see often enough, as well as the neighbors. Thinking of new ways to gather and perhaps ringing the changes can really lift the season. Last year everyone in our small cul-de-sac swapped the usual festive get-together for an outdoor winter solstice party. We lit a brazier and toasted marshmallows for the kids, while the adults got merry on a steamy saucepan of mulled cider. Everyone brought mince pies, and armed with lanterns and a few improvised instruments, we huddled together and sang carols beneath the stars. It might have been disastrous had the weather turned, but in fact it was a mistuned but magical highlight we plan to repeat.

Unless we're super chilled entertainers, parties can end up adding stress at this time of year—though there's no need to go over the top with our hospitality plans, because at Christmas especially, people come and go in their very best festive spirits, whatever's on offer!

If the mammoth organizational task of hosting a large party is not for you, there are alternative ways of seeing friends and family on a more intimate scale, which I confess I prefer—perhaps a crafty coffee morning or an afternoon tea. As a way of involving the children, we might organize a cinema trip with friends to see a new Christmas film, followed by tea and a gingerbread-decorating session.

TIP
FOR ANY SPECIAL EVENTS OR BIG BASHES, NOW IS THE TIME TO SEND OUT "SAVE THE DATE" EMAILS OR CARDS, AHEAD OF GETTING INVITATIONS AND DETAILED ARRANGEMENTS IN PLACE.

CHRISTMAS PARTY CHECKLIST

DATE, TIME, AND INVITATIONS

Check best friends' availability and that there are no major date clashes.

Send out "save the date" messages six weeks in advance.

Follow up with invitations which include any dress code/theme, the address, and directions.

Be sure to include public transport information and details of parking arrangements.

NOTES

GUEST LIST

ORGANIZE IN ADVANCE

Book musicians/DJ/music kit.

Book caterers or pre-order food.

Hire any specialist equipment, e.g. tables, chairs, tableware (crockery).

Order drinks and hire glasses.

Organize any help you might like on the night (which will free you up to mingle).

Think about decorations and lighting.

Speak to neighbors (perhaps with an invitation!).

THINK OF ONE DISTINCTIVE ELEMENT OF SURPRISE YOU COULD
ADD TO YOUR PARTY TO MAKE IT UNIQUE OR GO WITH A BANG!

DRINK

Consider pre-making punches or cocktails in jugs.

FOOD

Think balance of flavors, textures, and
colors—making it all in advance avoids stress!

Remember any special dietary needs.

AHEAD OF THE DAY

Clean the house.

Clear space for coats and find extra coat hangers.

Sort out music or playlists.

Organize any games and activities.

Pack away any fragile or valuable items and off-limits
alcohol!

Put together an emergency bucket with carpet cleaner/
stain remover/scrubbing brush/cloths/paper towels.

Stock up on toilet paper.

Put out hand towels and soap.

Set up lighting (indoor and outdoor) and candles.

Set out spare garbage bags.

Place ashtrays outside for any smokers.

Make plenty of ice, including frozen citrus slices.

If necessary, borrow extra refrigerator space from friends
or neighbors the day before.

Consider best layout of furniture, food, and bar area.

Order any fresh flowers for the day.

Book a hair appointment for yourself and plan your outfit.

Write out detailed timetables for cooking and tasks on the day.

PARTY FOOD

HONEY MUSTARD SAUSAGES

In a large sheet pan, place 1lb/500g cocktail sausages, toss in 2tbsp/30ml oil and roast at 400°F/gas mark 6/200°C for 20 minutes. Transfer the sausages into a big bowl with a mixture of 3tbsp/45ml honey and 3tbsp/45ml wholegrain mustard. Coat sausages evenly and return to roasting tray and oven for 5 more minutes. Serve with cocktail sticks.

Make twice as many as you think you'll need—they're everyone's favorite by miles!

BRIGHT AND BEETIFUL DIP

In a food processor, blend 2 cups/300g cooked beetroot with 1tbsp/15ml olive oil, 2tbsp/30ml lemon juice, 2/3 cup/150g ricotta, a crushed garlic clove, ½tsp each ground cumin and coriander, and salt and pepper to taste. Serve with a scatter of pumpkin seeds and a medley of raw vegetable sticks and tortilla crisps.

SPICED NUTS
(makes 5-6 jars)

In a large bowl whisk 2 egg whites and 1tbsp/15ml cold water until frothy. Toss in 6 cups/ 750g mixed unsalted nuts (e.g. walnuts, hazelnuts, almonds). Make up a spice mix of 1tsp sea salt, 2tsp each of ginger and cumin, 1tsp cayenne pepper, ½tsp dried chili flakes, 2tbsp finely-chopped rosemary, and 2tbsp/30g light brown soft sugar. Coat the sticky nuts in it thoroughly, then spread on two lined baking sheets and bake for 20 minutes at 350°F/gas mark 4/180°C, turning over halfway through to prevent scorching and ensure they are evenly golden. Allow to cool and store in an airtight container. Garnish with rosemary sprigs to serve. They're great for gifts too—everyone loves these nuts!

WARM olives are sublime—pop them in the oven at 325°F/gas mark 3/165°C for a few minutes and serve!

HOT ARTICHOKE AND CHILLI DIP

Delicious with crusty bread—and makes a great starter (for 8) baked in individual ramekins, too.

Mix together 2 cans of artichoke hearts, 1 cup/200g grated Parmesan cheese (keep back 1tbsp), 2tbsp/30ml mayonnaise, and 3 chopped green chilis (without seeds!). Transfer to an 8-in/20cm round baking pan, sprinkle over the reserved Parmesan, and bake at 350°F/gas mark 4/180°C for 15 minutes.

ICED grapes
look gloriously wintery
on any platter and are always
devoured—freeze them the
night before and take out
just before serving

PLATTERS can be brought together in a flash—charcuterie, pickles, chutneys, cheeses (hard/creamy/gooey/smelly/crumbly) served with crackers, breads, walnuts, Medjool dates, iced grapes, and Concorde pears (which don't brown too quickly), cut horizontally just before the party starts for stylish effect.

AND SOMETHING A LITTLE SWEET...

Make a platter of cookies, nuts, and pieces of fruit with a sweet dip or two.

Dot bowls of chocolate coins, sugared almonds, or clementines around the place.

WHITE CHOCOLATE DIP

Stir 9oz/250g melted white chocolate (slightly cooled) into 1¾ cups/400ml whipped heavy (double) cream with 1tsp vanilla extract.

GINGER MASCARPONE DIP

Using a fork, beat 2 finely-chopped balls of stem ginger and 2tbsp/30ml of its syrup into 1 cup/250g mascarpone.

FESTIVE DRINKS

CRANBERRY AND ORANGE SPARKLER

Pour 21oz/600ml tonic water, 7oz/200ml cranberry juice, and 7oz/200ml orange juice onto lots of ice in a jug. Add gin to taste (or leave out for drivers!). Garnish with cranberries and rosemary.

POMEGRANATE PROSECCO

Add 1tsp/5ml elderflower cordial, 1tsp/5ml pomegranate seeds, and a small sprig of rosemary to each glass, then fill with chilled prosecco.

MULLED CIDER

For every 2pt/1 liter of hard cider, add 4oz/120ml brandy, the thinly peeled zest and juice of 1 orange, 2 cinnamon sticks, 2tbsp/30g dark brown soft sugar, 4 cloves, and 1tsp vanilla extract. Heat gently in a pan on the hob for 20 minutes or more, then serve.

OR   Substitute 1pt/500ml cloudy apple juice and 1pt/500ml ginger ale for the hard cider, for a yummy nonalcoholic version.

Garnish each glass with a slice of apple cut horizontally.

KEEP IT SIMPLE

Impromptu get-togethers can have the highest *hygge* factor and the lowest levels of hassle; how about a Sunday brunch for a family or two, which is not such a big deal as lunch, but still a treat, or a pajama party for children with Christmas storytelling, and hot chocolate topped with whipped cream and marshmallows?

Mrs BSD Christmas from Illinois has a great social arrangement with a group of her best friends, which never varies—they all put dates in their diaries to watch *A Christmas Carol* at her house to kick off the season, followed by small gatherings in each home, to see one another's decorations and exchange small gifts—but only once Thanksgiving has passed. Right now, they are all busy preparing for those celebrations later in November, largely focusing on tasks in the kitchen and decorations absolutely everywhere! Mrs BSD Christmas chooses Thanksgiving decorative elements that can easily become festive ones. Among the orange pumpkins, she makes sure she includes a few of the rarer white variety, which she'll later arrange with poinsettias and other greenery especially for Christmas.

HOMEMADE GIFTS

Every Christmas it's my intention to celebrate in a more personal way—making more and shopping less. I'm near evangelical in pushing the "homemade" concept to the young—which in practice means my own children and their friends. As a wiser and older Mrs Christmas, I implore you to help your little ones make presents and decorations for the house and their bedrooms, so that creating things will always inform their sense of festive occasion; add in cups of hot chocolate and baked treats and it'll be something they want to repeat every year.

Around now, I start looking through magazines and books, and scanning websites, to find inspiration for making very simple gifts, even if they will just be small additions to a bought present, or a handmade embellishment to add to the wrapping. Receiving something that someone has taken the time and trouble to make for us, no matter how simple or small, is heartwarming in a way store-bought gifts cannot match. Mrs ER Christmas recalls a deeply touching gesture by her Uncle Arthur on Christmas Day, 1946. Just after the war, when toys and materials were scarce, he built her a dolls' house from old tomato crates. The chimney stacks were cotton reels, the bannisters were made of matchsticks, and the whole house and its contents were full of thought and love. Last Christmas at a vintage fair, I came across an old polished walnut, carefully divided in two, lined in silk and given the tiniest imaginable brass hinge and clasp to keep it shut. It cradled a tiny china baby swaddled in a grubby piece of flannel. I held the walnut tight, toying with owning it or not, wondering who had made it and for whom, what joy it had given, and how Christmas was celebrated that unknown year.

Making presents ourselves can be time-consuming of course. A few years ago, my teenage son spent all of Christmas Eve out in the garden sawing and

TIP
IMMERSING OURSELVES IN REAL PREPARATIONS THAT FOCUS OUR SENSES AWAY FROM THE MASS-PRODUCED AND GENERIC CONNECTS US TO THE TRUE SPIRIT OF GIVING AT CHRISTMAS.

An album of photographs.

A knitted cotton dishcloth in festive stripes.

A basket of cheese with a jar of homemade relish (see page 37).

Felted decorations or festive-shaped coasters/mats cut from old sweaters (100% wool) shrunk on a hot wash.

A child's knitting/crochet bag or wood-carving kit with a tutorial promise.

Hair scrunchies from fabric offcuts—or a bow for the cat's collar.

Plant cuttings or planted bulbs in lovely pots.

A cowl, fingerless gloves, hot water bottle cover, or tea or coffee cozy made from recycled knitwear.

A toweling hairband with a homemade facial scrub or mask.

A bottle of fizz and some homemade blackberry liqueur (see page 23).

A bird-feeding hamper with homemade fat balls.

Edible gifts galore (see pages 124 and 125).

hammering, forging fallen branches and greenery he'd foraged into a decoration for our porch. His big sister, meanwhile, was busy knitting me a gift, armed with some fine merino wool and a YouTube tutorial; on Christmas Day, with great ceremony, I was presented with a beautifully tissue-wrapped and beribboned package containing just one sock, with a promise of the other one another year!

Mrs EG Christmas likes to be a little better prepared. She sews all of her presents every Christmas, and starts planning the making of them in early fall. Her essentials are some good audio books and a very sharp stitch unpicker, she confesses. Her top tip is to choose one item that will suit everyone (such as washbags or table runners), and vary the colors or the fabric to suit each recipient's tastes.

COOKING AHEAD

Turning to tasks in the kitchen and having cleared space in my freezer, I make a concerted effort this month to double up on quantities when I'm making family meals. Half of whatever I'm cooking—casseroles, curries, chili, sauces, and pie fillings—can then be bagged up and frozen. This means that on days when I'm out at Christmassy events or just extra busy come December, there are weekday meals ready and waiting. This week I also aim to make some extra freeze-ahead one pot dishes and soups in larger quantities for visitors. These will be versatile enough to stretch to however many mouths might need feeding in the coming weeks, just by adding in extra ingredients or a few side dishes.

Arguably eating beef should only be an occasional pleasure, so I have included a very festive and delicious recipe for Cranberry Beef Casserole, which is also a handy freezer standby.

BOTH THESE SOUPS HAVE FABULOUS FESTIVE COLOR—FOR AN EASY ALTERNATIVE GARNISH, SERVE WITH LITTLE STARS (OR OTHER SHAPES) CUT FROM A BUTTERED TORTILLA WRAP, SEASONED AND FLASH FRIED!

PORKY PEA SOUP
(serves 8–10)

In a large pan, gently sweat 4 chopped rashers of bacon and 1 chopped onion in 2tbsp/25g butter for about 10 minutes. Add 3 cups/500g frozen peas, 2pt/1 liter of ham stock, ½tsp sugar, and seasoning to taste. Liquidize with a hand blender. Swirl in cream to serve.

CREAMY SPICED SQUASH SOUP
(serves 8–10)

Chop 1 onion, 1 butternut squash (unpeeled but de-seeded), and 1 sweet potato cut into 1-in/2.5-cm cubes. On a roasting tray, toss in 2tbsp/30ml oil, 1tsp salt, 1tsp chili flakes, and 2tsp mixed spice. Roast at 400°F/gas mark 6/200°C for 1 hour. Cool, then blend in a liquidizer with 2pt/1 liter vegetable or chicken stock. 2tbsp/30ml marsala and 1tbsp/15g mascarpone. Season to taste, then scatter on crumbled blue cheese and toasted pumpkin seeds to serve.

SIMPLE SOUPS AND A WINTERY STEW

CRANBERRY BEEF CASSEROLE
(serves 8)

In a large, flameproof casserole dish, heat 2 tbsp/30ml oil and sear 2½lb/1kg braising steak (cubed) in batches. Remove to a plate, add more oil, and sweat 2 finely-chopped onions, 4 crushed garlic cloves, and a finely-chopped 2-in/5-cm piece of fresh ginger, until soft. Return meat to pan and add 2tsp ground cinnamon, 1½tbsp/25ml harissa paste, 2tbsp/30g ground almonds, 3 bay leaves, and 5 cups/1.2 liters beef stock. Bring to a boil then place in the oven at 300°F/gas mark 2/150°C for 2 hours, adding ¾ cup/100g chopped dried cranberries 10 minutes before the end of the cooking time. * Serve with festive couscous and chopped parsley.

* If freezing, omit cranberries and add after fully defrosting, before you reheat.

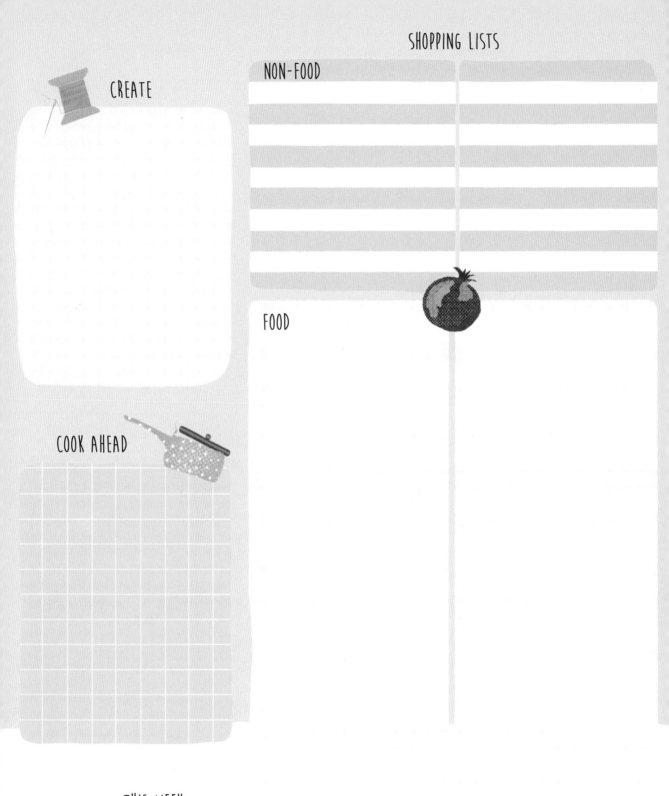

CREATE

SHOPPING LISTS

NON-FOOD

FOOD

COOK AHEAD

THIS WEEK: *Book babysitting or hairdressing slots now for popular Christmas dates. Start thinking about your wardrobe, too.*

EAT

ORGANIZE

MON

TUES

WEDS

THUR

FRI

SAT

SUN

HOST

EARLY
NOVEMBER

CHAPTER 5

MID-NOVEMBER

"The fruit and the spices were intended to represent the offerings of the Wise Men. The ... suet was the 'horned cattle' in whose stable the Saviour was born."

WRAP IT UP

By mid-November I'm already wrapping presents to keep on top of the task. If it is left too late, wrapping can become a painful and uncreative chore, so I start early and wrap in dedicated diary sessions to keep it entirely pleasurable. Mrs CH Christmas sets up her ironing board low in front of the TV as a wrapping table and watches something Christmassy at the same time—a marvelous idea to borrow, particularly if, as in my house, clear surfaces are hard to come by at this time of year.

Beautiful wrapping need not be complicated or expensive. If I have recycled well from last Christmas, and collected bags, boxes, and other scrap stuff throughout the year, then I may not actually need to buy very much in the way of wrapping materials at all—other than a stash of tissue paper, a roll of plain wrap, or a single sheet of something special.

Somewhat indulgently, I own a permanent "wrapping station" on wheels in which I keep all my wrapping stash, so I can move it to wherever I want to wrap—in front of the fire after children are in bed, or tucked away in secret. It arose by chance. Father Christmas once gave my two little daughters a wooden toy shop with tiers of beautifully crafted crates full of groceries. When my youngest daughter was about six, she decided to go for a change of use one Christmas time, turfing out the exquisite edibles and in their place depositing bits of card, wrapping paper, labels and stickers, lengths of string and ribbon, foraged feathers, and felt tips. There must be a gene. Then she'd park herself by the window with a coloring book, and wait patiently for us all to turn up with our Christmas gifts for her to wrap for a small sum. She was thrilled with her profits; in return, we had extraordinarily distinctive gifts covered in copious quantities of tape and wild embellishment. After a few years she passed her wrapping shop on to me and I've had it ever since—though I've ditched the customers.

WRAPPING IT UP

TAPE

Heavy-duty and sharp-edged dispenser (so it can be used with one hand), good-quality clear and invisible sticky tapes, double-sided sticky tape and dispenser, and washi tape—either to use decoratively or temporarily for writing on, to identify a wrapped present waiting for its finishing touch.

SCISSORS

2 pairs of long-nosed paper scissors (tie one pair to something permanent so they never go astray), a scallop-edged variety, and some sharp fine-nosed small ones.

MISCELLANEOUS

Hole punches, label cutters, glue sticks and glue gun, craft wire, and card.

KEEP A PAPERCLIP UNDER THE ENDS OF ALL TAPE FOR INSTANT ACCESS!

MY WRAPPING STATION

PAPER

Rolls of brown and colored kraft paper, half reams of tissue, cellophane (preferably the biodegradable kind), a sheet or two of special paper (I love hand-blocked designs), which can be used for small touches so that it goes a very long way (as can last year's salvaged wrap—see pages 56–57). I have a bag of shredded wrap to use as stuffing in gift bags and boxes, and lots of tulle, muslin, and fine fabric for wrapping, too.

OUTSIDE THE BOX

Colorful containers can be used to wrap many things—no need to disguise them, merely to enhance in a festive way—and spread the recycling word! Wooden boxes make fantastic little hampers for edible gifts, either left plain or painted in chalky emulsion, and lined with parchment.

LABELS

I make these through the year, by recycling old Christmas cards and wrap. I also keep a box full of inks, and metallic, gel, and paint pens for writing on them.

WRAP A CONE

Cut out semicircles of thick wrap, wallpaper, triple layers of tissue, or newspaper between cellophane, then twist around to form a cone and tape in place. Line with parchment if filling with edible gifts—add a tie, topper, and label.

RIBBON

Tie or decorate using ribbons, baker's twine, string, raffia, embroidery thread, or shredded strips of recycled fabric.

WRAP A BOX

Anything soft or irregular in shape is easier to wrap when it's put in a box. Cutting the paper to the correct size gives the best result. Roll the gift along the wrap to work out the width and add 2in/5cm for overlap. The length should be the same as the length of the gift plus an extension at each end of a little less than the gift's height. For a professional finish, crease the paper sharply wherever there is a fold, and turn over raw edges for a crisp line. I use double-sided tape for an invisible finish, though normal tape can be hidden by ribbons or other ties.

height

length

width

EMBELLISHMENTS

Old beads, buttons, paste jewelry, and bits and bobs from the natural world—dried seed heads, pine cones, and acorns (which can all be attached by wire or hot glue gun). I make sleeves, bows, 3D shapes, and stars from scrap paper (see pages 154-155), or at the last minute I add some fresh greenery. A candy cane or lollipops are great for children's gifts.

Mrs Nimble Christmas buys plain strong paper bags in a selection of sizes. She pops in a present, then folds over the top of the bag and secures it with a sticky label. No precision and no sticky tape needed.

Giving money or a voucher? Place inside a larger-sized matchbox covered in a band of wrap cut to its precise length and secured with double-sided tape...

OR MAKE A SPECIAL PULL-OUT SLEEVE:

Take one thick envelope and chop off one short side, creating a semi-round recess in the middle. Decorate with a band of wrap.

ONE VOUCHER
beer/lunch for two/trip to the sales/cinema and popcorn/flowers/ chocolate, etc.

Next, create a piece of card to slide inside. From the same wrap, cut out 2 small circles, fold in half and slot over each end. Punch a hole through the three thickness and thread through a small piece of ribbon. Either write your gift details directly on to the card, or wrap a voucher/bank note in tissue that is the right size to tuck under both semi-circular tabs. Slide into decorated envelope and add a label.

Make bands of wrap to seal around a gift inside a recycled box, or wrapped in tissue, newspaper, or plain paper, and finish with a ribbon. Make a bow embellishment using a square of paper; fold up in concertina style to create pleats. Pinch in the middle and tape on a thin contrasting piece of wrap. Or make simple paper snowflakes which look lovely atop gifts—all perfect for children to create too!

Why not make some gift bags with scraps of wrap too (see opposite)?

SCRAPS OF WRAP

SCRAPS ARE ALWAYS USEFUL, WHETHER FROM AN EXTRA SPECIAL SHEET OF PAPER OR FRAGMENTS SALVAGED FROM LAST CHRISTMAS.

Partially cover label-shaped pieces of card with patterned paper or use up tiny scraps of paper to make a patchwork effect. You could also use a craft knife to cut out letters of the alphabet—the easy ones—from card for a more personal touch.

FANNED LABEL

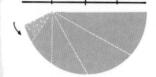

Cut a semicircle of wrap. Starting one-quarter of the way along the bottom edge, fold one segment back on itself at an angle of about 30 degrees.

Continue to fold backward and forward in concertina style, keeping each folded angle identical to create a tree shape. Punch a hole in the point of the tree and thread ribbon through to attach it to a gift.

TOILET ROLL TUBE PILLOW POUCH

Cut wrap as high as (a) and twice as wide as (b) with a ½-in/1-cm overlap.

Flatten the cardboard tube and lightly score curves at each end with a craft knife or scissor edge. Cover the outsides of the tube in glue, and press on wrap with glued overlap in the middle of one side. When dry, place gift inside and gently press in the ends.

For simple-shaped presents (or soft ones rolled into a lozenge shape), wrap in brown paper, tissue paper, or even pages from magazines. Encase the wrapped gift in a strip of wrap the same width, placing a blob of glue on the bottom of the wrapped gift to hold in place. Fold over the ends at the top. Punch holes, and thread ribbon through them to secure.

Use a plain paper bag with top folded down and glue on a wrapping paper "label" to seal. Punch a hole (or two) in the top and thread through ribbon. Add an embellishment.

STOCKING TIME

Mid-November is the time for getting serious about helping Father Christmas. In our house, stockings form the most significant element of our presents—though a large part of their contents will be day-to-day items which might otherwise have been supplied during the year. We all have our own stocking, made to last our lifetimes; my mother still puts out her stocking for Father Christmas, which was made by her mother during World War Two from a remnant of blast net, which was hung over windows to protect against flying glass from bomb damage. According to family legend, when he was a small boy, my father's stocking once contained nothing but a single piece of coal, presumably because Father Christmas felt that was what he deserved. We daughters never dared to discuss his precise transgression, since the very notion of such horrifying festive retribution was enough to keep us silent. Secretly though, we hoped it wasn't really true, or if it were, that Father Christmas only applied his strict rules to boys.

To wrap or not to wrap is a pertinent question when it comes to stockings. In Mrs NW Christmas' house, Father Christmas upholds her eco-friendly approach and never wraps his presents. In ours, if only to slow down the process and enhance the anticipation, they all come tissue-wrapped by Santa, either in different colors or stamped with an initial to ease the sorting on his sleigh. Having observed his ways as both child and parent, I believe his aim is to foster a sense of magic (how did he know how much I hoped for this? need that? love them?)—or at the very least elicit a quietly chuffed response to a small selection of pleasing presents. A smattering of guilty or restricted pleasure can elevate the opening of a stocking to giddy heights; when we were very young, my sisters and I adored finding a toy candy store one year, full of jars and scoops and weighing scales and multiple bags of candy—and one each!—when sweets were always for sharing and a rationed treat the rest of the year. At the age of eleven, my daughter was thrilled to find a very high-heeled pair of red glittery shoes in her stocking, which she knew we'd never have permitted. Groundbreaking technology always has the power to delight too. In the late 1950s, Mr AD Christmas found a Walt Disney slide projector in his stocking, which could make Mickey Mouse and eleven Disney friends appear on his wall when he closed the curtains and flicked the switch. Some sixty years later, he still remembers that sublime Christmas morning joy.

FATHER CHRISTMAS LIKES TO CREATE A CAREFULLY COMPOSED SELECTION OF PRESENTS...

A STOCKING MIGHT CONTAIN SOMETHING...

...TALL AND ENTICING POKING OUT OF THE TOP!

- umbrella
- cooking utensil
- bottle
- long chocolate bar
- candy cane
- shoe horn
- back-scratcher
- rolled up comic or magazine

...THAT YOU

- need
- wear
- drink
- share
- desire
- eat
- read
- play with
- make or do

...AND IN THE TOE

- pomegranate
- chocolate money
- Christmas underwear
- lucky charm
- candies
- lottery ticket
- satsuma
- nuts

...THOROUGHLY

- indulgent
- forbidden
- free
- practical
- sentimental
- shocking
- nostalgic
- frivolous
- daft
- charitable

For children, make-believe outfits or role-play presents are always welcome, and a crafty kit goes down well whatever our age—from villages for worms to ginger-beer making. Father Christmas often pops in something highly practical too: Mr JB Christmas found the softest radiator brush in his stocking last year; and Mrs SS Christmas's son pulled out a most thoughtful rubber plunger, after a year of blocked lavatories in his college student rooms. Whatever the composition or scale, Santa knows the secret to a cheery stocking is its thoughtful tailoring to the owner's unique tastes. And he certainly does not source his goods from any store insensitively promoting "stocking fillers," may I add in an indignant tone!

STIR-UP SUNDAY

At the end of this week sits the last Sunday before the beginning of Advent, known in the UK as "Stir-Up Sunday." This is when the Christmas pudding (see opposite) is traditionally made, though in our kitchen, we take all weekend and start with the Christmas cake (see page 65). I follow a recipe given to me by brilliant baker Mrs SB Christmas, but Mrs Nimble Christmas likes to ring the changes by baking hers to a simple and very flexible recipe.

Until just a few years back, I didn't make a pudding at all because of all the steaming palaver, instead buying one from a local fair or school bazaar. I don't especially like having an over-steamy kitchen or having to worry about checking water levels in the steaming pan. But all that changed when I discovered the overnight method of steaming a pudding—a delightful revelation. It needs just half an hour steaming on the hob and then, as long as I have my timings right, it goes into a low oven just as it's time for bed. And don't be put off by what seems like a complex recipe; it all just sloshes together and really is simple.

A TRADITIONAL BRITISH CHRISTMAS DESSERT, MADE WITH DRIED FRUIT AND STEAMED.

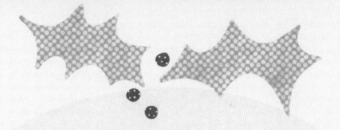

FOR THE PUDDING

Serves 8–16 depending on appetite!

Morning In a large bowl place 3 cups/450g dried fruit of your choice, ¼ cup/50g mixed peel, 3 chopped balls of stem ginger and 1tbsp/15ml of its syrup, the zest and juice of 1 orange and 1 lemon, 1tsp mixed spice, a pinch of salt, ½ cup/125ml Pedro Ximenez sherry, and ⅓ cup/100ml stout (dark beer). Mix well and cover with a dishcloth (teatowel).

Evening Simply stir into the soaking mixture ¾ cup/150g dark brown soft sugar, 1½ cups/150g shredded suet, 1¾ cups/100g breadcrumbs, ½ cup/75g self-rising flour, and 2 beaten eggs. **Gather everyone in the house to stir the pudding mixture and make a wish!** Put the mixture into a well-buttered 3-pt/1.5-liter pudding basin (or divide between two smaller basins) and cover with a pleated double layer of waxed (greaseproof) paper with foil on top. Tie tightly with string, leaving one end long to create a string handle. Half an hour or so before bedtime, put it in a large ovenproof pan with a well-fitting lid, with a trivet inside to raise the pudding off the bottom. Carefully add boiling water to the pan, to come halfway up the side of the basin. Bring back to a boil and simmer on the hob for 30 minutes. Then transfer the whole pan with pudding inside to a non-fan oven at 250°F/gas mark ½/130°C for 10 hours (or 8 hours if you make two smaller puddings) while you sleep! The next morning, remove the pudding from the pan and when cold, turn out and double wrap it in fresh paper, foil, and string.

To serve Warm 1tbsp/15ml brandy in a metal ladle over a flame. Tilt slightly to ignite and then carefully douse the pud in it.

STORE THE PUDDING IN A COOL, DARK PLACE UNTIL CHRISTMAS.

In the morning, the whole house is filled with Christmassy aromas and I turn the pudding out with a huge dollop of happy satisfaction. When it comes to Christmas Day, it can be steamed for an hour in the oven in the same way. I have been known to put our half-sized one in an the microwave, which doesn't seem to do it too much harm (half-sized because I generally make two puddings from one mixture—one for us and one to give away if we don't have lots of visitors with us on the big day).

In the nineteenth century, Mrs Christmases (many of whom would have been servants) would probably have set aside whole days for the task of making mincemeat and baking Christmas puddings. Suet—the hard fat of beef or mutton—could only be bought from the butchers, and needed finely chopping by hand. For candied peel, orange peel was steeped and simmered in sugar water, then baked and minced. The only almonds which were generally available, or indeed affordable, had to be shelled, blanched, then skinned. Raisins and currants were laid out on the kitchen counter, sprinkled well with flour, then rubbed between fingers to remove both stalks and dirt. Pips were then removed—a slow and sticky old business—working each and every little pip upward toward the stalk end. Back in 1865, it all seemed to be done without any sense of it being laborious:

"Now the preparation of the mince-meat was a solemn ceremonial, in which no careless or inexperienced person was allowed to take part. The weighing and chopping, the grating and stirring, were affairs carried on with closed doors, and an amount of mystery which made us youngsters regard a mince-pie as something almost sacred, though not too sacred to be eaten with relish… 'Cousin Hetty' … told me how the fruit and spices were intended to represent the offerings of the Wise Men; the meat and suet the 'horned cattle' in whose stable the Saviour was born; and the oval tins in which the pies were baked, the manger in which He lay."

A PIECE OF (CHRISTMAS) CAKE

ANOTHER BRITISH TRADITION, THIS FRUITCAKE IS
EATEN THROUGHOUT THE HOLIDAYS. HERE'S A RECIPE
FROM MRS NIMBLE CHRISTMAS, TO ADAPT AS YOU
FANCY WITH DRIED FRUIT AND NUTS OF YOUR CHOICE.

START THE NIGHT BEFORE YOU PLAN TO BAKE THE CAKE.

Makes one 8-in/20-cm cake.

Overnight *Soak 6⅓ cups/950g mixed dried fruit in 5tbsp/75ml brandy and the juice of 2 oranges and 2 lemons, plus all their zest.*

The next day *Cream together 2 sticks/250g of softened butter and 1¼ cups/250g light brown soft sugar until pale and fluffy. Gradually beat in 4 eggs, then 1tbsp/ 15ml molasses (black treacle). Fold in 2tsp mixed spice, 1⅔ cups/200g all-purpose (plain) flour, ¾ cup/100g chopped nuts, the dried fruit, and any remaining soaking liquid. Transfer the mixture to a lined 8-in/20-cm round, deep cake pan. Wrap the sides of the pan in a double layer of brown paper, and tie in place with string. Cover the top of the cake mixture with a double layer of baking parchment, with a 1-in/ 2.5-cm hole cut out in the middle. Bake in the oven at 300°F/gas mark 2/150°C for around 2½ hours or until a skewer inserted in the middle of the cake comes out clean. When cold, pierce the surface of the cake and dribble a tbsp of brandy over it (to be repeated weekly). Double wrap the cake in fresh paper, foil, and string, and store in a cool, dark place until nearer Christmas (see page 127 for how to decorate the cake).*

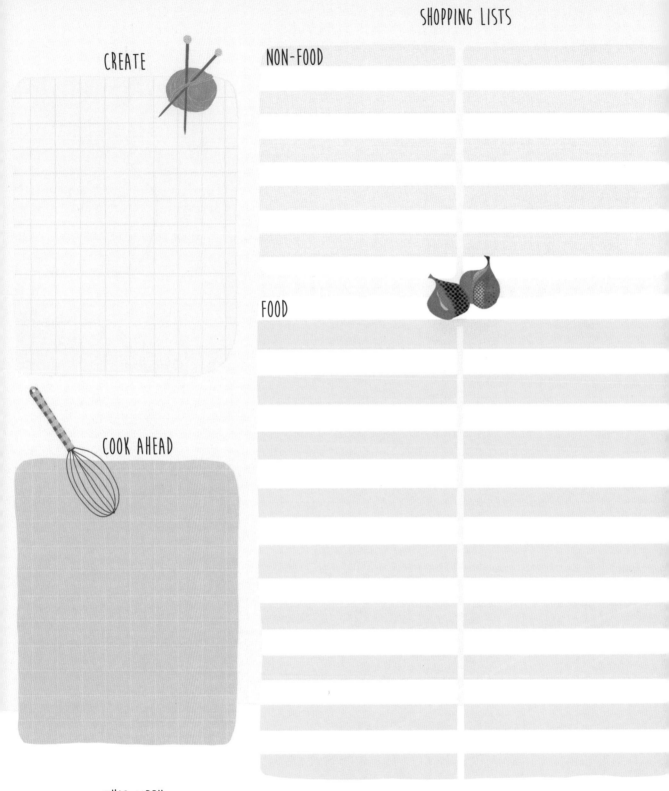

CREATE

SHOPPING LISTS

NON-FOOD

FOOD

COOK AHEAD

THIS WEEK: *Print photos and compose letters to send with your Christmas cards. Buy postage stamps.*

 EAT

MON

TUES

WEDS

THUR

FRI

SAT

 ORGANIZE

SUN

HOST

 MID-NOVEMBER

CHAPTER 6

LATE NOVEMBER

"What counts is not the method, but that the festive message isn't rattled off without love or proper thought..."

SEASON'S GREETINGS

I am now on the final stretch of gathering and wrapping presents, especially those I need to post or exchange well ahead of Christmas. A priority this week will be getting my Christmas cards sorted. Perhaps we should heed the advice given to *Good Housekeeping* readers back in 1925, to steer clear of the "hell" of post offices next week, due to "people obediently Posting Early"! Starting sooner on cards could be wise—especially if you are like Mrs CS Christmas, who includes handwritten letters with hers, inside lavishly embellished envelopes. Mrs AS Christmas creates more time to write personal messages (along with a family photo) inside her cards by using printed address labels, instead of addressing the envelopes by hand. These special touches are so far removed from impersonally and hastily scribbled cards—surely a waste of time, temper, and earthly resources?

I'm not sure e-cards are the answer either, because although they tackle the issues of waste and cost, they are by their nature impersonal. As a thoughtful solution, Mr and Mrs CJM Christmas email a beautifully curated collection of wintery photos they've taken themselves. Might a scan of a child's drawing or some family photos taken during the year work equally well? What counts is not the method, but that the festive message isn't rattled off without love or proper thought; or in the case of the classic "round robin," too much trumpet-blowing— which is at best highly entertaining and at worst plain dull.

Mrs Nimble Christmas suggests abandoning Christmas cards altogether and simply sending just a few New Year's cards out after Christmas to those who would cherish them. Most people won't even notice!

CHRISTMAS CARD LOG

TO	ADDRESS			

TO	ADDRESS			

FOOD FOR THOUGHT

What we might eat this Christmas begins to occupy my mind around now. In our house we try to have a special menu-planning session at the kitchen table. With a glass of something red in hand, we browse through recipe books and any notes we have made at previous Christmases, and chart out what we would like to cook over the coming weeks. Christmas for some is a time to push the culinary boat out, but I find the best way to avoid stress is to keep food simple and prepare most of it in advance, using tried and tested recipes I have to hand. Setting up a recipe reference log from our cookery books saves time as we begin planning and compiling our shopping lists.

I find it helpful too, to keep a record of ingredients I always need to buy at Christmas, listed out by shop or shop-type—and of everyday items that are easily forgotten in busy times or dwindle fast when the house is full. Alcohol and toilet roll come under that same category! Our food shopping and feasting are wildly extravagant, I know—we are celebrating after all—but planning properly does at least cut down on food waste. And shopping with a few eco-friendly principles in mind slightly eases my seasonally flaky conscience…

PLANET-FRIENDLY FOOD SHOPPING

- Write meal plans and shopping lists to avoid over-buying and food waste.

- See pages 88–89 for suggestions of foods with a particularly long shelf life or versatility over the holidays.

- Cook your own festive food if you can and buy less ready-made, processed food (with the right recipes, it can be more delicious, more rewarding, and simpler than you think).

- Avoid plastic packaging if possible and if not, always check if it is recyclable (and reuse when you can).

- Be air-mile conscious and buy local, seasonal produce.

- Shop locally and support stores that sell loose, unpackaged food—take your own bags and a selection of containers.

- Embrace imperfect produce to reduce waste.

- Keep to hand good recipes for leftovers—and use your freezer rather than binning any excess.

FAVORITE RECIPES

RECIPE	BOOK/AUTHOR	PAGE	NOTES

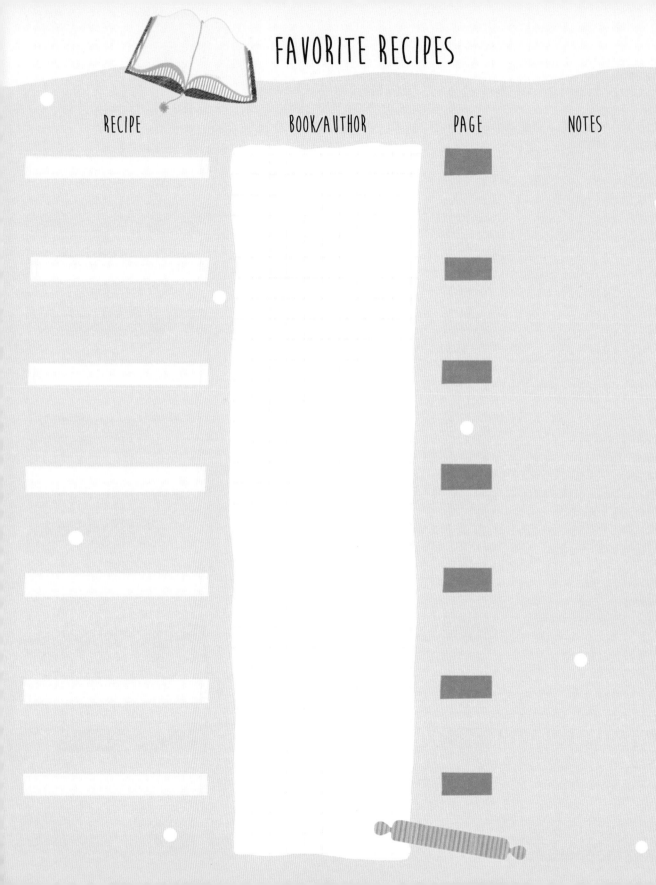

WHY NOT ORGANIZE YOUR RECIPES INTO CATEGORIES?

RECIPE	BOOK/AUTHOR	PAGE	NOTES

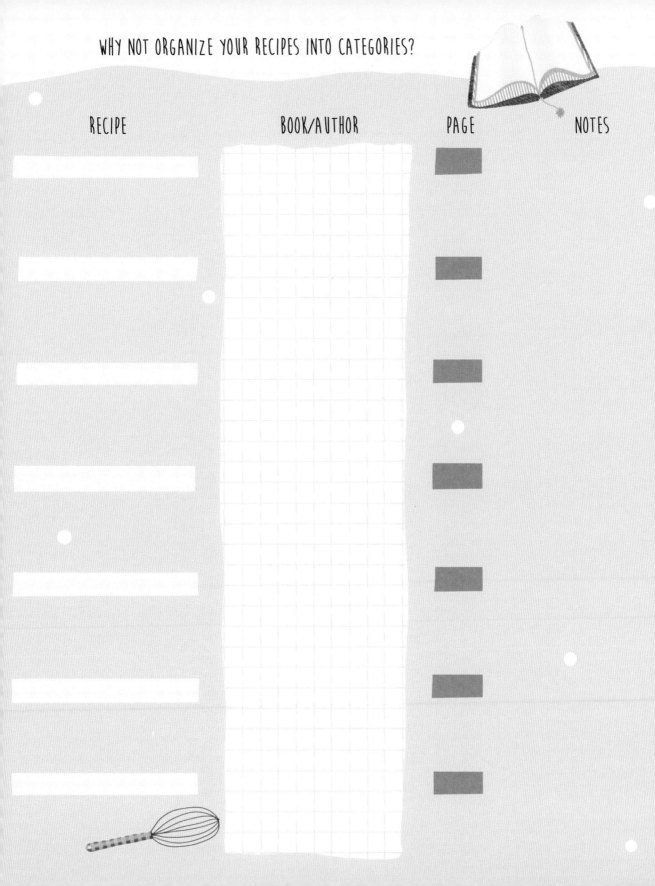

SHOPPING REMINDERS

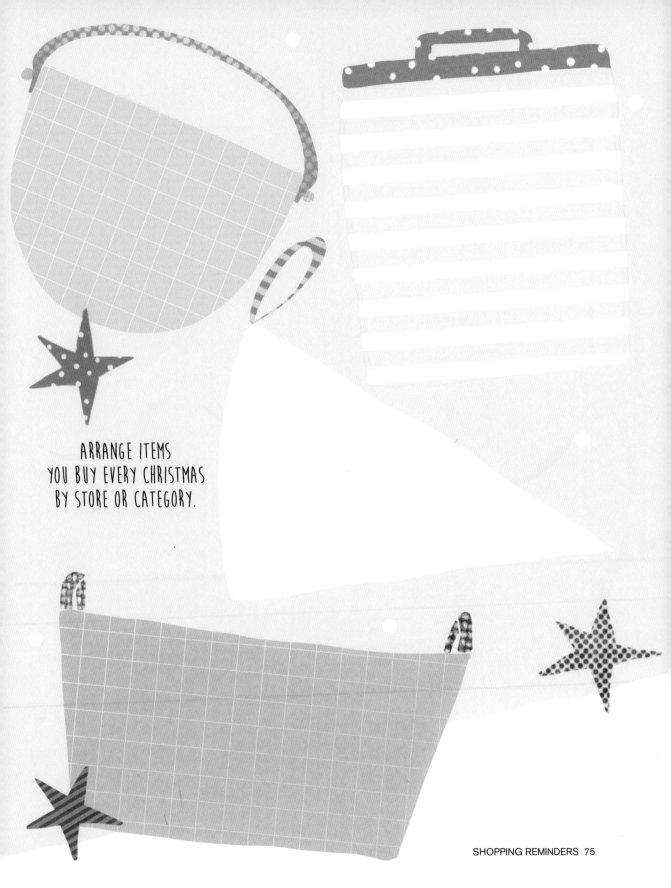

ARRANGE ITEMS
YOU BUY EVERY CHRISTMAS
BY STORE OR CATEGORY.

ADVENT

Now's the time to think about Advent, which we'll start to celebrate soon. In Germany, Mrs HW Christmas buys boughs of bluest spruce to create an advent wreath with ribbons and four fat candles nestled into them, to be lit in turn on the four Sundays of Advent. Also in Germany, *Weihnachtsmarkt* (Christmas markets)—held throughout Advent in the main town or village square, and often featuring a spectacular nativity scene complete with live animals—are getting ready to open. These markets are a guaranteed delight for the senses, with heavenly aromas of spiced wine and gingerbread—and my favorite, *Reibekuchen* (deep-fried grated potato cakes) with apple purée—a once-a-year treat only!

Advent calendars are popular in many countries, so gather yours together now, or their contents if you are making a homemade one. Mrs AG Christmas has a fine fabric one with pockets, which she brings out year after year for her boys to share. It's the kind of piece which you could make yourself earlier in the year if you're nifty with the sewing machine. Far simpler is propping a store-bought one up at the breakfast table (with a gesture of surprise, please!). Mrs SK Christmas strings up a ribbon and pegs on it mini zinc buckets or little bags with a small treat in each.

A KINDER CHRISTMAS

Ramping up kindness to others in the approach to Christmas heralds and celebrates the season like nothing else. Our local clergyman and his wife have a sign in their driveway, just off a fairly narrow road, which reads, "You are very welcome to turn around here." Every time I pass it, even though I've never needed to take up their generous offer, I feel the warmth of its message. Reaching out to one another should of course be a year-round habit, but perhaps at Christmas it feels more valuable than ever.

For many of us, Christmas is a time when we feel the loss or absence of loved ones most keenly, as well as sadness for the kind of Christmas we may never have again. If you happen to be on your own for Christmas (or part of it, like many parents who are separated or divorced will be), open your mind to contacting a charity that might welcome your help as a volunteer for a few hours. Or invite friends, family, or neighbors who might be lonely into your house. Thoughtful communion with others is relevant to every size and shape of family, friendship group, or neighborhood. At this time of year, even Mrs Humbug Christmas starts to warm up a bit.

It's kindness more than any other step that makes the whole festive song and dance worthwhile. Mrs MS Christmas often made her adored grandmother an advent calendar using old photographs taken during her long lifetime (which were copied from albums belonging to wider family or friends, some of which her grandmother had not seen before). Mrs MS Christmas placed each photo inside decorated and numbered envelopes and then propped up them up all over her grandmother's house—surely a heartwarming (and interactive!) idea for younger and older generations to share. This can take a little research, but the immense pleasure and fond recollections that photographs can generate are worth every moment of thought and effort.

Pop a lottery ticket in a Christmas card for someone who deserves some good luck!

Offer a carer or parent with a young child a few hours off and step in to help.

Tonight, make each member of your household an extra special bedtime drink.

Help a child make their own Christmas gifts or take them shopping.

Buy a homeless person something they may need, such as a toothbrush, or gloves. Do ask them first.

Arrange a surprise Christmas grocery delivery for a loved one.

Send an anonymous contribution to someone who might like some help with Christmas expenses.

Take the dog for an extra-long walk— yours and/or someone else's.

Visit a care home to play board games, or read or chat to someone with no visitors.

Put aside half an hour and phone a faraway friend or relative who lives alone.

Treat someone special to a home facial, massage, manicure, or pedicure.

Donate to a charity that organizes extra support for people in need at Christmas time.

Write a long newsy letter to an elderly friend or relative and enclose a photo.

Set up a regular direct debit to a charity—every little helps!

Send (or deliver locally) Christmas flowers or a plant to someone special.

Buy a hot drink for a charity fundraiser out on the streets.

Tip the people who deliver your post or newspaper, or collect your trash, or anyone else who's there all year.

Fill a stocking for someone deserving to open on Christmas morning.

Make a donation to a food bank or supermarket food collection point.

Offer to be chauffeur to someone who does not drive or have a car.

Give blood (for free!).

Put birdseed or fat balls out in the garden—and don't forget water, too!

Schedule a diary date in January with someone you've not seen all year.

Invite someone who has made a difference to your life this year over for tea and cake.

ADVENT CALENDAR OF KINDNESS

DIVIDE IDEAS BETWEEN FAMILY AND FRIENDS FOR A HEARTWARMING DECEMBER—WHY NOT DEVISE YOUR OWN?

COMMUNAL CALENDAR FOR ADVENT

How it works Three or four friends each send out this invitation
to two or three people in the local community in mid-October, asking
them in turn to invite one local friend or neighbor each, to join
in too. Everyone will gather in mid- to late November to exchange
small Advent gifts.

INVITATION

PLEASE JOIN OUR GIANT GROUP ADVENT CALENDAR

To: _____   From: _____

A Create, source, or buy—then wrap (in a similar way) four small gifts* labeled
from you and marked 1, 2, 3, and 4.

B Please bring them to a Christmassy coffee on _____ (date)
at _____ (address)
the home of _____ tel: _____

C All gifts will then be redistributed so we each receive four, marked 1, 2, 3, and 4,
from different donors, to open on the four Advent Sundays before Christmas.

*Gifts can be identical or not—something recycled or handmade, knitted, sewn, or
baked—a charity shop find—or a mini gift—not exceeding _____ in value.

SWEET THINGS

Around now, Mrs AS Christmas makes mini pudding-shaped chocolate fondants to put in her freezer ready for Christmas. No-one in her house much likes Christmas pudding, so with a sprig of holly popped on top of each, these are a fun alternative on Christmas Day. Her recipe leaves her with plenty of spare egg whites which she turns into tiny pavlovas, which also freeze well—once defrosted, they make the basis of an instant dessert at any time over the holidays.

I like to freeze a couple of desserts too—the very act pleases the Mother Hen in me, knowing I can easily feed my Christmas chickens with something sweet! I often make a large iced cheesecake and then a couple of ice cream bombes— one to serve as an alternative to Christmas pudding on Christmas Day, and the other there to slice into whenever an instant dessert is required. I have a versatile recipe for ice cream which requires no fancy ice cream maker and in its plain vanilla form works really well with hot mince pies and spiced or caramelized fruit. Last year I froze some in a vintage metal loaf pan, which was great for serving straight from the freezer. Here I include the most delicious pecan pumpkin pie ice cream, inspired by a recipe from Mrs SF Christmas of Connecticut, who uses ingredients left over from her Thanksgiving dinner to create a very special treat, in popular demand every Christmas.

ICED LIME CHEESECAKE

Line a 2lb/1kg loaf pan with foil that extends 4in/10cm above the height of the pan. Into its base press the combined mixture of 1 cup/150g crushed digestive biscuits and 5tbsp/75g melted butter. In a large bowl, whisk to soft peaks ⅞ cup/200g cream cheese, ⅔ cup/150ml heavy (double) cream, 1⅓ cups/300ml condensed coconut milk (normal is fine, too), and the zest and juice of 3 limes (this may take 5 minutes). Spoon on top of the biscuit base, cover loosely with the excess foil, and freeze. Remove from the freezer 20 minutes before serving and scatter with pomegranate seeds.

This can be made with lemons or oranges instead of limes. You can also freeze the mixture and scoop out little balls with a melon baller which can be turned into snowballs by rolling them in desiccated coconut and putting them straight back in the freezer until required.

CHOCOLATE AND CHESTNUT BOMBE

Mix 4tbsp/60ml rum with 1¼ cups/150g crushed amaretti biscuits. In a separate bowl, whip 1 pt/500ml heavy (double) cream to soft peaks and then fold in 1 cup/225g sweetened chestnut purée, ⅔ cup/100g chopped chocolate, and the amaretti mixture. Rinse a 2-pt/1-liter pudding basin (don't dry inside), fill, and freeze. When ready to decorate, melt 1¼ cups/200g chocolate and stir in ⅓ cup/100ml heavy (double) cream. While the chocolate is cooling, dip the bombe basin in very hot water and turn the bombe out on a plate. Swirl the melted chocolate all over, then return to the freezer. Remove from the freezer 20 minutes before eating—stick in a sprig of clean holly (with its stem covered in foil) to serve.

ICE CREAM

Simply beat (to soft peaks) 2⅓ cups/600ml heavy (double) cream, a 14-oz/400-g can of condensed milk, and 2tsp vanilla extract. This may take 5 minutes! Stir in extras of your choice (see some suggestions here), then freeze.

Cranberry swirl—Simmer 1 heaped cup/100g fresh cranberries with 3tbsp/45ml water and ¼ cup/50g sugar for 5 minutes. Completely cool then swirl through the ice cream. Children love this with a big handful of mini marshmallows stirred in.

Chocolate ginger—Stir through 1tbsp/15ml stem ginger syrup, ½tsp ground nutmeg, 4 balls of finely chopped stem ginger, and ⅔ cup/100g dark chocolate, chopped into small chunks.

Pecan pumpkin pie—First make some caramelized pecan crumbs. Combine 3½tbsp/50g melted butter with ½ cup/100g superfine (caster) sugar, ⅓ cup/50g chopped pecan nuts, 3 cups/200g brown breadcrumbs, and 2tsp cinnamon, then spread out on a baking sheet. Bake at 350°F/gas mark 4/180°C for 20-25 minutes until deep golden brown, turning midway through to prevent burning. Bash the toasted clumps with a rolling pin to break them up and, when cold, stir into the ice cream, along with ⅔ cup/150g canned pumpkin.

CREATE

SHOPPING LISTS

NON-FOOD

FOOD

COOK AHEAD

THIS WEEK: *Sort out any dry cleaning you'll need for the party season, and start thinking about festive playlists (or finding your CDs!).*

EAT

ORGANIZE

MON

TUES

WEDS

THUR

FRI

SAT

SUN

HOST

LATE NOVEMBER

CHAPTER 7

VERY EARLY DECEMBER

"Other than the gentle falling of snow, sadly not within our powers to command, candles have the most magical impact going."

SETTING THE SCENE

The whole month of December is as fundamental to my festive pleasures as Christmas Eve and Christmas Day themselves. If I have been broadly on target with my November lists, then from now on, all things frantic are banished. Any new lists do not extend beyond December 23rd—though isn't that the day specifically scheduled by children for suddenly coming up with the ultimate present they'd like more than anything else in the world?

Woman's World magazine in 1925 declared now was the time to start fattening our geese for Christmas, varying their diet between potato parings, barley meal, ground oats, and rendered waste meat fat, in order to keep their appetites healthy. A decade later, readers of *Wife and Home* were reminded to ensure their stoves were gleaming clean, ahead of all the Christmas cooking—given a mother's role was to ensure that her cooking met with full approval from the whole household.

I'm rather more interested in my decorations: making my kitchen table look Christmassy in time for Advent and styling my front door. Mrs VS Christmas usually makes a door wreath (there are all kind of instructions online) over coffee with friends. Stylish Mrs RH Christmas, who lives out in the country, once made an exquisite door wreath entirely of pheasant feathers. And Mrs Nimble Christmas ties a branch of two of greenery and a pine cone to her door knocker, which serves just as well.

In our front garden we have a pair of standard holly trees, clipped into balls and perfect for draping in tiny solar-powered outdoor lights. These come on as daylight fades and give me a ridiculous amount of pleasure. On the front porch, we have permanently fixed galvanized wire to the underside of the tiled roof. Each year we attach tied swathes of birch twigs (which I reuse every year) to the wire, and thread fresh greenery through them. Out of my garden shed comes a long length of jute rope with pine cones tied to it at intervals, exactly the right length to frame my front door. Long lengths of ivy, bunches of holly, and a few decorations can then be attached to the rope. I might dig out a galvanized lantern or lean an old wooden sleigh I have against the house, add some warm fairy lights, and gather together some pretty pots filled with moss and white cyclamen or hellebores.

You may prefer decorative daftness like my sister Mrs MW Christmas, who clearly has more Disney DNA in her than I do! She has a pot-bellied Santa figure who sits on her doorstep and bellows "ho ho ho!" (when his motion sensor is activated) at smiling passers-by. If your tastes are more subtle, you could always find a pair of topiary plants, or smart outdoor lanterns with candles to grace either side of your entrance. Mrs KS Christmas, who lives in an apartment near Cologne in Germany, always decorates her window boxes with strings of fairy lights for Advent. Whatever your space or style, the key for me is having fitments (the hooks, nails, etc.) already installed, and gathering any "props" in one place, rather than trying to source everything from scratch when you need it.

CANDLELIGHT

The answer to ornamental success indoors, according to Constance Spry, the famous mid-century British royal florist, was a minimalist approach and concentration on pockets of decoration, rather than aiming to cover a whole room. Perhaps she would have approved of my initial efforts at decorating which I begin in earnest now, simply using candlelight—intimate, inviting, and full of *hygge*. Other than the gentle falling of snow, sadly not within our powers to command, candles have the most magical impact going. A good few bags of tea lights went on my shopping list last week, the eight-hour variety in particular, which (in the UK, at least) conveniently last from when darkness creeps in until it's time for bed. They live in my candle drawer (you might have guessed I had one), which I try to stock up during the year when I come across ones I like, along with a pile of long cook's matches, candle holders, snuffers, and saucers. There's no need to buy too many candle holders, as everyday household items can be drafted in—cake stands or jelly molds, platters, upside down bowls, and, best of all, mirrors underneath (and behind) for stunning effect. Clusters of candles look fabulous, using different colors, heights, and widths—though at the dining table, either very tall displays or low (even floating) groups of candles work best of all.

DECK THE HALLS

When it comes to scented candles, quality outweighs quantity to my mind. I like to indulge in the same favorite one year after year. In one posh glass jar, it is the essence of Christmas in our house. Other aromas can equally revive forgotten memories of Christmas past, whether that's festive baking or the scent of freshly gathered greenery, one of the most ancient customs of all. As far back as we know of, people have decked their halls with boughs of holly, ivy, rosemary, and mistletoe, with spices, rosy red apples, and oranges being added to the mix. In 1865, one delighted little boy described how he and his cousins were allocated the customary task in their home, of sticking a "holly-leaf with a shining berry on its point" on every small latticed window pane of their drawing room.

Mr CTM Christmas gathers vast swathes of holly and ivy to wrap around the beams in his living room, which used to be an old barn. Because it's lofty and doesn't get too hot, the greenery lasts well, whereas in my more confined home it needs changing every few days. We tend to have one great forage outdoors and then keep our evergreen bounty in a large sack by the back door, ready to replace any fading pieces.

TIP

REALISTIC ARTIFICIAL GREENERY IS PRETTY PRICEY, BUT A ONE-OFF INVESTMENT. I COMBINE IT WITH THE REAL THING (IN SUCH A WAY THAT FRESH PIECES CAN BE EASILY REPLACED), TO MAKE AUTHENTIC-LOOKING ARRANGEMENTS THAT DO NOT WILT IN MOMENTS ON THE MANTELPIECE OR OTHER WARM PLACES.

Around now, I begin to think about any store cupboard and refrigerator or freezer ingredients I can buy this far in advance, to spread out the task of festive food-shopping—for ourselves and for guests we plan to invite round. Over the years, I've developed a list of long-life and versatile ingredients which can sit on standby and be used throughout the busy month of December, ensuring we can always rustle up a good few meals—without having to plan anything specifically.

A NIMBLE KITCHEN

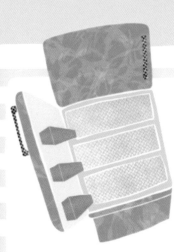

FREEZER

Frozen lemon and lime slices for drinks

Frozen berries for breakfast, hot and spiced with ice cream, or served frozen with melted white chocolate drizzled over

Good vanilla ice cream

Frozen peas for pea and ham soup or pasta with pancetta, leftover turkey, and creamy cheese sauce—great for children, too!

Sausages—best butcher's (cocktail size too) and vegetarian ones, to serve for main meals or as party bites

Breadcrumbs, brown and white, made from leftover bread, ready for Christmassy recipes

Ice cubes containing sprigs of herbs and pomegranate seeds or a cranberry

Ready-rolled puff pastry for cheese straws, quick tarts (both sweet and savory), and pie tops

Chopped herbs packed into ice cube trays for cooking (not garnishing)

Write your own customized lists of what you find most useful to have in your own refrigerator and freezer...

In the freezer:

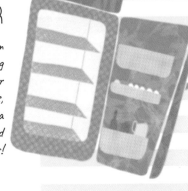

REFRIGERATOR

Filtered milk with extra-long shelf life · aerosol cream for hot chocolate and pancakes · cream cheese (including a herby garlic variety) · halloumi and feta cheeses for salads and lunches · dried French and Italian sausages, salami, and chorizo, ready to slice thinly for a charcuterie board · pancetta or bacon in cubes and slices · plenty of eggs!

STORE CUPBOARD

In the refrigerator:

All kinds of chutneys and relishes, especially caramelized red onion—great for making a sticky sauce for sausages, with goat cheese for canapés, and with charcuterie

Nuts of every kind, for eating, garnishing, and sprinkling on salads and desserts

Tins of sweet chestnut purée for simple desserts including "Mont Blanc" made with whipped cream

Long-life milk as a back up to the supply in your refrigerator

Brioche and fruited panettone for breakfast on its own, as cinnamon toast, or made into a dessert—lasts for ages

White and dark chocolate, for eating, drizzling, dipping, and making sauces

Floured tortilla wraps make good lunches as quesadillas or easy pizza bases, as well as wraps

Jars of pickles and olives for platters and general nibbling

FRESH FRUIT AND VEG

In addition to fruit and vegetables for specific meals, I stock up on longer-lasting and versatile ingredients to use from before Christmas into the new year.

Lemons and red onions for everything!

Clementines to eat and for salads (sweet and savory)

Melons and pineapple for breakfasts

Pomegranates for display, garnishes, and salads

Apples and pears for munching, salads, and cheese boards

Figs, which I buy unripe, for salads, breakfast, or caramelizing for a dessert

Red and white cabbage and Brussels sprouts on a stalk for Christmas coleslaw and salads, or to sauté with pancetta

Parsnips, sweet potatoes, and butternut squash for roasting or making soups

BAKING BEGINS

At school, children are really focusing on Christmas by now, decorating their classrooms, making surprises to bring home at the end of term, and rehearsing for special concerts and performances. Little ones all over mainland Europe will be excited about putting their shoes, clogs or boots out the night before December 6th, in the hope St Nicholas might fill them with sweets and small treats. Mrs Christmas will be helping him out there. Once I'd have been busy sewing costumes for the school play, or getting messy with the children at home. Mine have always loved baking Christmas biscuits or *Plätzchen*, as they are called in Germany—a taste of childhood for me, when we lived next door to a bakery there. From the beginning of Advent, the baker's windows were always stuffed with marzipan figures, gingerbread houses, and these very traditional biscuits which come in a multitude of shapes.

In homage to those long-ago visions, I generally bake a few varieties using different kinds of nuts. I make a plainer dough too, that can be formed and frozen, ready for slicing and baking (straight from the freezer) at a moment's notice. My adaptation of a shortbread recipe is inspired by some very dear Italian family friends, who once gave us tiny sugar-smothered biscuits called *angeliche*, which are unimaginably Christmassy and melt like snowflakes on your tongue. My version of them is perfect for offering to unexpected friends who might pop by at teatime—Mrs Humbug Christmas, please do!

SHORTBREAD TWO WAYS

Cream together 2 sticks/200g softened unsalted butter with ½ cup/100g superfine (caster) sugar. Mix in 1⅓ cups/200g all-purpose (plain) flour and ¼ cup/50g semolina to form a dough.

Petticoat tails: Press the mixture into a greased 10-in/25-cm round cake pan and bake at 300°F/gas mark 2/150°C for 50–60 minutes. Remove from the oven and prick the surface with a fork to make a pattern, then cut into 12 wedges. Remove from the pan when cold.

Snowflakes: Form 3 sausages from the Shortbread dough (1in/2.5cm thick) on separate pieces of plastic wrap, and freeze. When ready to bake, take straight from the freezer, cut into ½-in/1.5-cm slices with a serrated knife, place on a baking sheet, and bake at 325°F/gas mark 3/160°C for 15 minutes. Remove from the oven and, when firm, lift them off the baking sheet. While they are still warm, coat them by gently turning them in a bowl of confectioners' (icing) sugar. Leave to cool.

SWEET BITES

ZIMTSTERNE (CINNAMON STARS)

Whisk 2 egg whites with a squeeze of lemon juice until stiff. Fold in ½ cup/150g sieved confectioners' (icing) sugar, then put 1 tbsp/15ml of mixture aside and loosen with a few drops of water to make egg snow for later. Mix in 3 cups/300g ground almonds and 1tsp cinnamon. Sprinkle some more ground almonds onto a board and roll out the mixture to a ½-in/1.25cm thickness. Cut out 1½-in/3-cm stars. Place on a lined baking sheet and lightly brush the saved egg snow on top. Bake at 300°F/gas mark 2/150°C for 15–20 minutes.

HAZELNUT MACAROONS

Stir up 2 unbeaten egg whites, ¾ cup/100g ground hazelnuts, ¾ cup + 2 tbsp/175g superfine (caster) sugar, and 1 tbsp/10g rice flour. With wet hands, roll into 1-in/2.5-cm balls and place them on a baking sheet spaced 1in/2.5cm apart. Poke a blanched hazelnut in the top of each ball. Bake at 300°F/gas mark 2/150°C for 30 minutes.

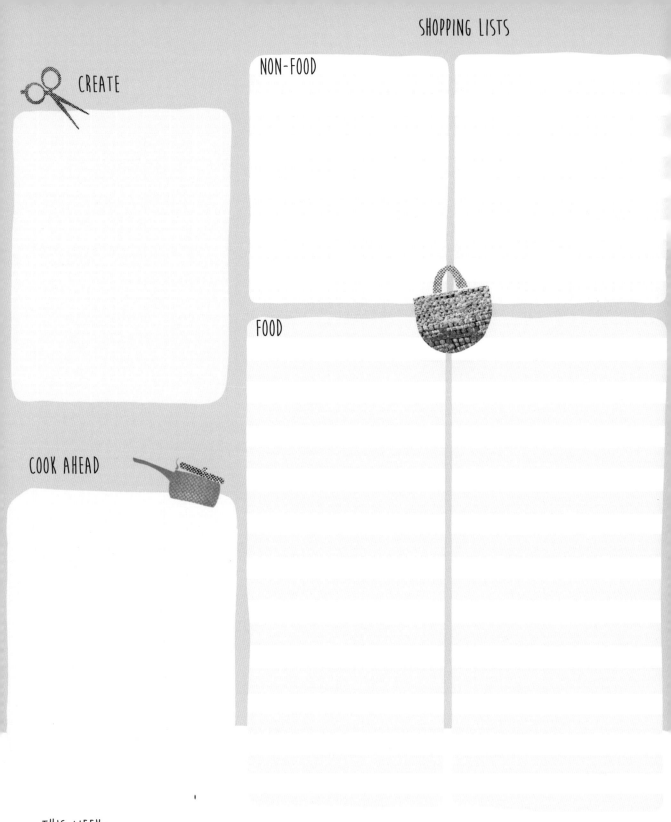

SHOPPING LISTS

CREATE

NON-FOOD

FOOD

COOK AHEAD

THIS WEEK: *Keep wrapping and remember to feed your Christmas cake! Think about any festive food orders, get out Christmas tea towels and tableware, and bring in any potted bulbs from the shed.*

EAT

ORGANIZE

MON

TUES

WEDS

THUR

FRI

SAT

SUN

HOST

VERY EARLY
DECEMBER

CHAPTER 8
EARLY DECEMBER

*"Christmas is the time for splendid theatricality,
pared-back sophistication, contemporary glamour,
and old-fashioned charm—ultimately, whatever
pleases us most."*

FINISHING TOUCHES

Over these next two weeks I gradually build up my decorations around the house, adding final touches until the very last minute to spread out the pleasure. I still recall tummy-churning excitement as a child, watching my father balanced on a stepladder, attaching brightly-colored concertina paper garlands to the ceiling and transforming our home into what felt like a Christmassy palace.

Around the corner from me *is* a Christmassy palace—it belongs to Mrs CS Christmas, a music teacher who works from home. She feels impelled to decorate every nook and cranny of her house bang on December 1st—all steps, stairs, surfaces, shelves, walls, and windows—such is the fervent appreciation she gets from her adoring pupils. It's gratifying to think their delighted wonderment now might inform their own Christmases one day, when they have homes of their own.

Like Mrs CS Christmas, I am not guided by fashion, theme, color scheme, or artistic direction when it comes to decorating the house, but simply by affectionate familiarity. The treasured pieces I've collected through the years probably look far more stylish in my own eyes than they are in reality, but who cares? I love natural materials but am easily tempted by a little glitz. I admire white and neutral palettes, but can't help being drawn to the warmth of deep reds, coppers, and oranges. I adore the cool crisp lines of Danish design, but then cannot resist my urge to include some charming vintage tat. Christmas is the perfect occasion for splendid theatricality, pared back sophistication, contemporary glamour, and old-fashioned charm—ultimately, whatever pleases us most.

For anyone pressed for time, the capacity of candlelight to transform a space is a real boon. Mrs Nimble Christmas suggests buying fewer but bigger candles, which last for ages and look extravagantly special. For additional decorative impact, place something bold and welcoming in the entrance to your home, such as a clear vase full of fairy lights, baubles, or sprays of twigs with berries on. A few festive potted plants like the Christmas rose are easy to dot around the place, too. Put out bowls of rosy red apples, limes, pomegranates, tangerines, walnuts, and bauble-bright foil-wrapped chocolates and your decorations will be adored.

GETTING READY FOR GUESTS

Mrs BSD Christmas gets out her Christmas wardrobe around now. She wears red, red, and more red, all the way to the big day—including coats, shoes, and bags. For now, the best I can manage is a red apron, perfect for the domestic chores which are calling me, particularly if we are expecting visitors this Christmas. I start by decluttering the hallway, moving all non-essential coats, hats, scarves, etc. elsewhere—under the bed is a good temporary space—and putting a large basket by the front door to hold shoes. If we're expecting overnight guests, I list who will sleep where and how many blow-up beds, pillows, sets of bedding, and towels we'll need for them. I find hot water bottles (the ultimate winter treat), coat hangers, a hairdryer, a non-ticking clock, some Christmassy magazines or books, a few toiletries, snuggly blankets, and toys if we're expecting any small children (making sure any cleaning materials are well out of reach, too). I also clear some drawer and hanging space and set out a low stool for luggage.

Over the next two weeks I make up guest beds and wash and iron spare sets of bed linen. Hopefully I'll have already ironed Christmas tablecloths, including one for a garden table we bring in as highly useful table-overspill space.

TIP
PLACE SOMETHING FESTIVE IN EACH VISITOR'S BEDROOM, EVEN IF IT'S JUST SOME SPRIGS OF HOLLY WITH BERRIES IN A SMALL VASE. THESE WILL LAST ALL THE WAY TO CHRISTMAS IF THE WATER IS CHANGED REGULARLY.

Depending on visitor numbers, we may need to find extra chairs, too. If we don't have enough tableware (crockery), knives and forks, and glasses, then I may ask visitors if they could bring some with them. Catering-wise, I find having faraway friends or family to stay most pleasurable when the main meals and puddings are largely prepared in advance. Mrs Nimble Christmas uses a few go-to recipes that are simply good combinations of great ingredients that can be brought together without skill or clever technique, ideally in just one bowl, saucepan, or roasting pan to minimize fuss and the washing up.

THREE NIMBLE BREAKFASTS

Christmassy French Toast (serves 8)

Cut 4 store-bought croissants in half horizontally. Make up a spiced egg mixture by whisking together 2 eggs, ⅔ cup/150ml light (single) cream, 1tbsp/15g superfine (caster) sugar, 1tsp cinnamon, and 1tsp mixed spice. Dip each croissant piece in the mixture, then sprinkle the cut sides with 2tsp light soft brown sugar. For every two pieces, add a knob of butter to a nonstick frying pan, and fry on a medium heat for 5–6 minutes, turning halfway through, until crisp and golden brown. Serve with Greek yogurt, red fruit compote (or berries, pomegranate seeds, and slices of blood orange), and a sprinkling of confectioners' (icing) sugar.

Festive Bircher Muesli (serves 6)

The night before, combine 1½ cups/200g rolled oats with ⅓ cup/50g finely-chopped dried cranberries or cherries, 1 tsp ground cinnamon, and 1¼ cups/300ml apple juice. In the morning, stir in 1tbsp/15ml milk to loosen, then 1 large eating apple, grated. Divide into bowls, then dollop on yogurt (or a decadent mixture of 2 parts Greek yogurt to 1 part heavy/double cream and a drizzle of honey, whisked to soft peaks) and a scattering of chopped nuts.

Creamy Smoked Salmon and Scrambled Eggs (serves 4)

In a large bowl, beat together 6 eggs, ¼ cup/50g cream cheese "chopped" into small pieces, 2 tbsp/30ml heavy (double) cream, and seasoning. Melt 2 tbsp/30g butter in a frying pan, then add the egg mixture and cook on a medium-low heat for around 4–5 minutes, stirring gently and adding ¾ cup/150g chopped smoked salmon and snipped chives to taste halfway through cooking. Serve with hot buttered toast or bagels.

THREE NIMBLE LUNCHES

1

Blue Cheese and Fig Pasta *(serves 4)*

Melt 1½tbsp/20g butter in a large frying pan and sweat 8 figs, quartered, for 4 minutes. Add the zest and juice of 1 lemon, a pinch of dried chili flakes, 2tsp finely-chopped rosemary, ⅓ cup/100ml heavy (double) cream, and ¾ cup/100g crumbled Gorgonzola or Dolcelatte cheese. Stir until all melted, then toss in the cooked pasta and serve with a garnish of chopped walnuts.

2

Naomi's Salmon Quiche *(serves 4)*

In a food processor blend 2⅓ cups/140g fresh brown breadcrumbs, ⅓ cup/50g hazelnuts, and 1 stick/110g softened butter. Press the mixture into the bottom and sides of a greased 10-in/25-cm loose-bottomed flan tin. Whisk together ¾ cup/200ml heavy (double) cream, 2 eggs, 1tbsp cornstarch (cornflour), and seasoning, then stir in 1 cup/100g grated cheese and 1½ cups/250g chopped raw salmon fillet. Pour into the case and bake at 375°F/gas mark 5/190°C for 30 minutes.

3

Speedy Savory Tarts *(serves 4)*

Cut 1½in/4cm off the short side of a ready-rolled puff pastry sheet (approx. 14 x 9in/35 x 23cm) and cut the remaining pastry into 4 equal rectangles. Score a ½-in/1-cm border round the edges of each piece and place on a lined baking sheet. Within the border, spread on 1 tbsp filling (see below), top with stars cut from the saved pastry, and brush the border and stars with milk. Bake at 400°F/gas mark 6/200°C for 15–20 minutes.

Filling A: 2 tbsp/30ml caramelized onion chutney mixed with 1tbsp/15ml water, 8 finely-chopped sage leaves, 6 slices prosciutto (chopped), and 1⅓ cups/100g sliced taleggio on top.

Filling B: 2 pears, sliced ¼in/0.5cm thick and sweated for 2 minutes on each side in 2tbsp/30g butter and 1 tbsp/15g brown sugar, 8 finely-chopped walnut halves, and ¾ cup/100g Roquefort cheese crumbled on top.

THREE NIMBLE MAINS

1

Turkey Thai Curry *(serves 4)*

Gently heat 1⅔ cups/400ml coconut milk, 1 cup/250ml chicken or turkey stock, 1tbsp/15ml Thai fish sauce, and 3 tbsp/45ml Thai curry paste of choice. Add 4 handfuls cooked turkey chunks and simmer for 10 minutes. Just before serving, stir in the juice of ½ lime and 6⅔ cups/200g baby spinach (which will rapidly wilt), and serve with rice, garnished with toasted almond flakes.

2

Stuffed Butternut Squash *(serves 2)*

Cut 1 butternut squash in half, de-seed, season, and drizzle with olive oil, then roast at 400°F/gas mark 6/ 200°C for 45 minutes. For the stuffing, sweat 1 finely-chopped red onion in 2tbsp/30g butter until soft, add 1 finely-chopped cooking apple, ⅓ cup/50g dried cranberries, ⅓ cup/50g roughly-chopped pecans, 2tsp/10ml maple syrup, and ½tsp mixed spice. Pile onto cooked squash and return to the oven for 10 minutes, then garnish with chopped parsley.

3

Festive Burgers *(serves 4)*

Mix together 1lb/500g ground beef (mince), 1 large finely-chopped onion, 1 beaten egg, 1tbsp breadcrumbs, 1 heaped tsp Dijon mustard, and 1tsp garam masala. Divide into 4 patties and roast at 450°F/gas mark 8/230°C for about 25 minutes, turning halfway through cooking time. Serve inside toasted brioche buns, with crispy bacon and cranberry sauce on top, and sweet potato fries and a creamy Brussels sprouts slaw on the side.

THREE NIMBLE DESSERTS

Chocolate and Chestnut Pots (serves 6)

Gently heat ¾ cup/200ml heavy (double) cream to simmering point. Off the heat, stir in 1 cup/150g finely-chopped chocolate. Once melted, add a 10-oz/250-g can of sweetened chestnut purée and 1tbsp liqueur of choice (such as Cointreau or Armagnac). Divide into 6 mini cups or ramekins and chill.

Sticky Cinnamon Figs (serves 4)

Pour 2tbsp/30ml honey into a hot frying pan, with 1tsp ground cinnamon and 1tbsp/15ml Pedro Ximenez sherry or marsala. Add 8 halved fresh figs face down (or try 4 pears, stalks and bases removed, cut in 1-in/2.5-cm horizontal slices) and cook for 5 minutes. Serve with ice cream or mascarpone and a sprinkling of chopped nuts.

Affogato (serves 1, repeat as often as required)

In each bowl place 2 gently broken cantuccini biscuits and drizzle with 1tbsp/15ml rum or brandy. Add 2 scoops vanilla ice cream, then "drown" in freshly made coffee (or hot chocolate without any alcohol for little ones). Serve sprinkled with grated chocolate.

OPEN HOUSE

I am never comfortable visiting friends' homes if we are doing all the relaxing and they are charging around and fraught, "entertaining" us. Delegating (and perhaps inviting guests to either bring a meal or simply help out) actually makes a visit more relaxing for everyone. My favored approach, learned from Mrs BW Christmas, is to choose food that enables visitors to help themselves as much as possible; at breakfast, perhaps put out a big bowl of fruit and set up a toast station; at lunch, a baked potato or bagel bar; how about an ice cream or hot chocolate station for the children, with aerosol cream, toppings galore, and sprinkles, replaced by a DIY cocktail bar for the adults later on? At any time during the holidays—visitors or not—getting everyone to help out eases any pressure and bumps up satisfaction levels and a sense of engagement in the whole festive process.

Keeping in a good selection of drinks to cater for everyone's tastes is near top of any hospitality list; drinks for children, sparkling water, and a selection of cordials for non-drinkers, plenty of beer in a few different styles, and some cider for mulling. We generally buy a few spirits (with all the necessary mixers) and a nice Armagnac—if there's any left after all the Christmassy cooking these last few weeks.

Now's a good time to work out what wine might be needed to serve with the meals being planned. Luckily for me, I live with a wine enthusiast, who has always taken charge of this bit of the preparations and suggests a few possible options for any Mrs Christmas who, like me, doesn't know her Chardonnay from her Shiraz.

CHOOSING WINE FOR CHRISTMAS

For an extra special splurge, think vintage Champagne made with extra love and attention from the fruits of one fine summer—a big step up in quality and worth the small hike in price every time!

Among the wine trade's best-kept sparkling secrets are Franciacorta from northern Italy and Cremant de Bourgogne (made just down the road from Champagne). Both give their posher French cousins a run for their money, as do the very fine fizzes which have emerged from England in the last decade.

FIZZ

Some of the very best Proseccos come from the region's sweet spot, Valdobbiadene—look out for its name on labels for drinking on its own, or if you're making Bucks Fizz or cocktails, most Proseccos are perfect.

DESSERT

Jewel-like golden Sauternes is as Christmassy as it comes, just perfect for taking to a festive dinner party. It is marvelous with fruit-based desserts and creamy dishes like crème brûlée or bread and butter pudding, but equally cuts the mustard with salty blue cheeses, fatty treats like chicken liver parfait, or even sweet-flavored vegetable dishes.

Vin Santo is worth seeking out. It pairs beautifully with mince pies, blue cheeses, and all things nutty, and Father Christmas is particularly fond of it in smaller bottles for poking in the tops of stockings belonging to wine enthusiasts. It goes without saying, then, that it makes a fabulous present for any epicurean, presented along with almonds, Italian biscuits, panforte, or dark chocolate.

WHITE

Pouilly-Fuissé or Viré-Clessé are both from the Mâconnais (in the sunnier south of Burgundy) and are just right for serving with turkey and trimmings on Christmas Day. They also have the weight to work wonders with Christmas Eve fish pie!

For a cold crispy dry aperitif, look no further than the wines from the Rias Baixas area of northern Spain.

Producers like Inama or Pieropan from the Italian Veneto offer very special Soaves which are nothing like the nasties of yesteryear!

Dry white classics go perfectly with festive canapés or starters. Happy couplings include Sancerre with goats' cheese or dry Rieslings from Germany, Alsace, or Austria with smoked salmon.

RULE NUMBER ONE IS TO BE GUIDED BY YOUR OWN TASTES, BUT HERE ARE A FEW IDEAS FOR ADDED INSPIRATION.

RED

A Cru Beaujolais (a little heftier than the summer-sipper Villages wines) or a Pinot Noir from New Zealand, California, or Chile work far better than big tannic reds, with fatty meals like goose or duck and likewise with turkey and the rich mélange of tastes at the Christmas table. These pair particularly well with charcuterie, gammon, and cold meat cuts after Christmas.

Made a big meaty casserole? Bring on those bolder reds from the southern Rhône, such as Gigondas or Vacqueryas, or a hearty Rioja or Ribera del Duero from northern Spain.

PASS THE PORT

It wouldn't be Christmas without cracking open a bottle of port. This year, why not try crusted port with your stilton? It's close in style to vintage port, but at a fraction of the price.

Don't overlook the much underrated aged tawny styles to go with your cheese and nut platters or mince pies. Or wrap it up as a gift to make a wine lover's Christmas Day!

SHERRY

Nutty, refreshing, and versatile, served ice-cold, dry sherry styles like Fino and Manzanilla are marvelous aperitifs and can be spot-on with starters or canapés like smoked salmon blinis or even cocktail sausages.

Amontillado sherry or the rarer Palo Cortado are smart choices with nuts, dried fruits, and hard cheeses.

Sweeter styles of sherry, like Oloroso, feed the Christmas cake beautifully and lift a Christmas trifle to mighty heights. They're perfect served alongside Christmas cake and with pumpkin, pecan, or mince pies.

Pedro Ximenez is even sweeter; sensational for soaking dried fruits destined for the Christmas pudding, thick enough to drizzle over vanilla ice cream, and one of the very few wines which can hold its own with a chocolatey dessert.

ROLL IT OUT

In the kitchen this week, I focus on all things pastry related. The making of mince pies (traditional British pastry tartlets containing mincemeat, a moist mixture of dried fruits and nuts) is non-negotiable. I usually make them small and shallow—partly because we like thin pastry, partly because it feels slightly less wicked to eat a whole stack of them, and partly because I'm useless at getting an intact batch out of deep tins. Mrs BH Christmas reminds me that it's vital we leave our cooked tarts in their tins for a good ten to fifteen minutes after they come out of the oven, so that the pastry firms, but remove them before they get stuck there.

Following the lead of Mrs RH Christmas, I batch-freeze large quantities of uncooked mince pies, still in their trays; then I take them out of the trays and transfer them into freezer containers in layers separated by baking parchment, so they can be lifted out in any quantity as I need them. At a moment's notice, I can put them back in the original tartlet tray in their frozen state for immediate baking. Most mass-produced pies simply do not compare, and these are truly worth the trouble—even with ready-made mincemeat, which I often buy if I've not got round to making some, tweaked with citrus to make it slightly less sweet.

And I always buy in plenty of ready-rolled puff pastry. Among other things, I use it for palmiers, which look exquisite but are the easiest thing in the world to knock up and freeze, ready to slice with a sharp knife and put straight in the oven from frozen, whenever you need a light bite to offer around. Mrs AH Christmas' family would not forgive her if she didn't make multiple trays of mince pies as well as her sensational sausage rolls—available all over the holidays, from freezer to table in a Christmas jiffy.

MINCE PIES

MAKING YOUR OWN PASTRY IS THE KEY TO MINCE PIE HEAVEN, AND IT'S SO EASY WITH A BLENDER

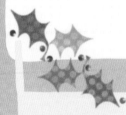

(makes approx. 24)

My mincemeat recipe is on page 156, but you could just add some citrus zest, brandy, and chopped nuts to a store-bought jar.

In a food processor, briefly process 2⅓ cups/300g all-purpose (plain) flour, a pinch of salt, 1 stick + 1tbsp/125g lard, 1½ sticks/175g cold butter, and 2 egg yolks until they form a dough. Wrap the dough in plastic wrap and refrigerate for 30 minutes before rolling out on a lightly-floured board to a thickness of ⅛in/3mm. Cut out approximately 24 circles with a cutter slightly larger than the holes in your tartlet tray, and place in the tray. Put a generous dollop of mincemeat in each case, then moisten around the top edge of the pastry. Using a slightly smaller cutter, cut out lids or stars and place on top of the mincemeat, pressing gently to seal around the edges. Brush the top of each mince pie with beaten egg, then bake at 400°F/gas mark 6/200°C for about 15-20 minutes (or 25 minutes straight from the freezer) until golden. Leave in trays to cool for 10-15 minutes, then remove to a cooling rack. Dust with confectioners' (icing) sugar to serve.

PASTRY

PALMIERS

A VERY HANDY BITE—SWEET OR SAVORY—READY TO BAKE STRAIGHT FROM THE FREEZER.

These are a doddle to make, using store-bought, ready-rolled puff pastry and any of the fillings below.

Whizz together any of the fillings in a blender and spread over a rectangular sheet of pastry (approx. 14 x 9in/ 35 x 23cm), painted with 1 tbsp/25g melted butter. Roll the short ends inward from either side until they meet in the middle, wrap the whole thing well in plastic wrap, and freeze. To bake, remove from the freezer for 15 minutes, cut with a sharp knife into ½-in/1-cm thick slices, and place on a lined baking sheet, leaving 1in/2.5cm space around each one. Brush with 1tbsp melted butter and bake for 10-15 minutes in a preheated oven at 410°F/gas mark 6-7/210°C. Remove from the tray and cool slightly on a cooling rack, then serve while still warm.

FILLINGS

Combine 1½ cups/175g soft blue cheese with ½ cup/75g chopped walnuts and 1tsp finely-chopped thyme leaves.

Combine ¼ cup/40g each of grated parmesan and finely-chopped salted pistachios.

Combine 2 tbsp/30g light soft brown sugar, 1½tsp ground cinnamon, and ¼ cup/40g finely-chopped pecans.

CREATE

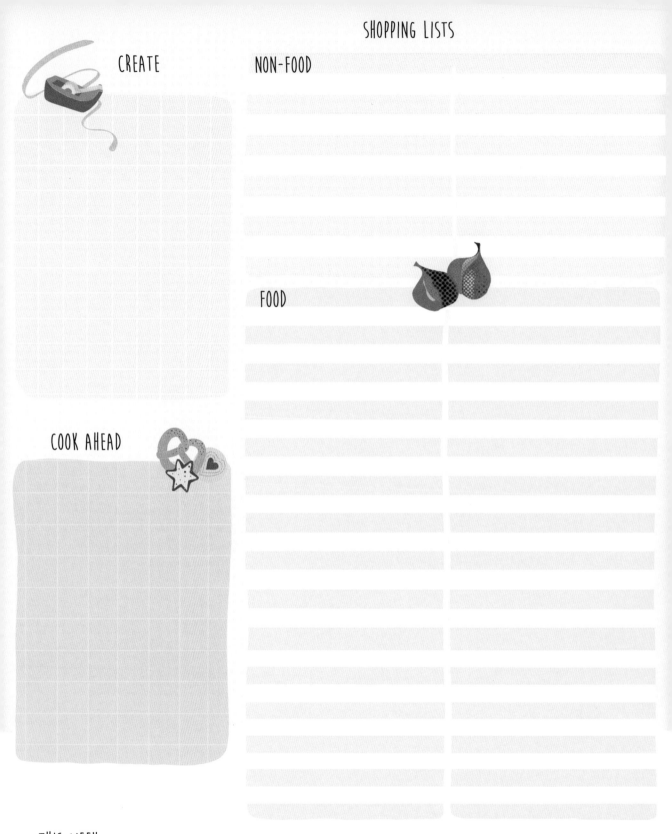

COOK AHEAD

SHOPPING LISTS

NON-FOOD

FOOD

THIS WEEK: *Keep wrapping and remember to feed your Christmas cake! If you are going away for Christmas, start your packing lists, arrange house sitting/pet care plans, cancel deliveries, and sort out security lights.*

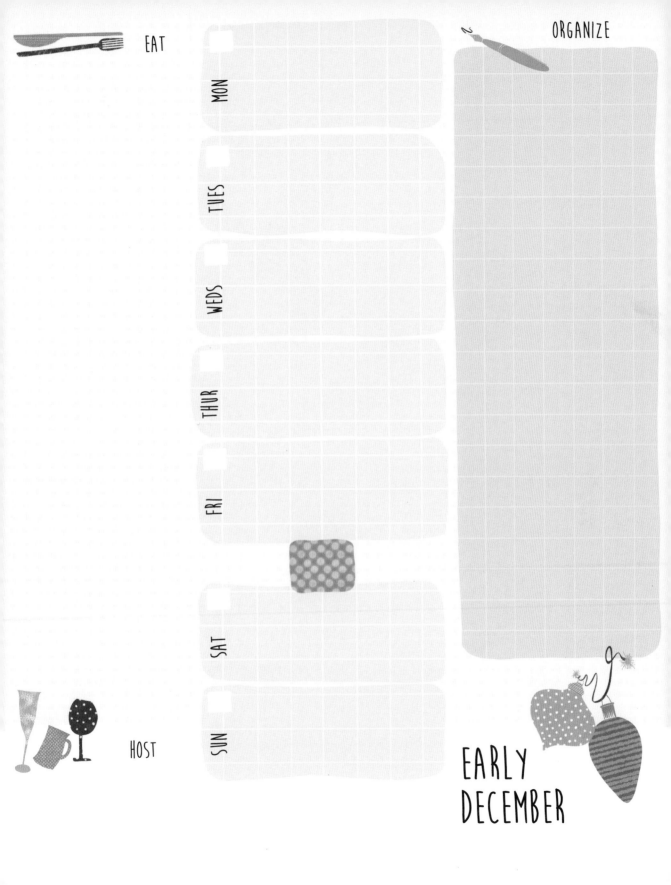

EAT

MON

TUES

WEDS

THUR

FRI

SAT

SUN

HOST

ORGANIZE

EARLY
DECEMBER

CHAPTER 9

MID-DECEMBER

"The ritual of rediscovering and hanging beloved decorations counts for far more than the esthetic and our tree is a reminder of every single precious Christmas we've ever had."

TREE TIME

Choosing our Christmas tree is a priority in early December. The hue is all important: darkest glossy green with a hint of blue is my ideal. Our living room has no space for a broad tree, much as I'd love one, so I hunt out an extra slim conical shaped one, with elegant symmetry, not too much density low down and no nasty gaps. And its branches must be plentiful high up—any lanky spurt of growth means an instant rejection! As she chooses which tree to cut down on the Pennsylvania Christmas tree farm she visits every year, the happy issues Mrs NB Christmas contends with are the snowy conditions and whether the trunk will be straight enough to fit in her tree holder.

How we decorate our trees is a private affair. There is choice and inspiration for exquisite Christmas tree schemes at every turn, unless you're a festive stick-in-the-mud like me, or Mr TJB Christmas who always uses his grandmother's vintage lights. The ritual of rediscovering and hanging beloved decorations counts for far more than the esthetic and our tree is a reminder of every single precious Christmas we've ever had.

Mrs BSD Christmas from Illinois adds one new decoration to her tree each year, always homemade, in the very same spirit as 100 years ago. Trees then were commonly draped in garlands of raisins or berries (or cranberries and popcorn in America). Foil from packets of tea or tobacco was made into bows, and monkey nuts covered in tissue were hung from the tree in place of expensive store-bought baubles. There is a true charm in handmade decorations for the tree; some years I have made simple miniature crackers to nestle among the branches.

If the very British ritual of pulling store-bought tacky crackers with their predictable jokes and trashy contents appeals, then simply skip this next section. I prefer to make my own crackers, because they're more personal and far lovelier than the poshest bought ones could possibly be. Mrs TB Christmas comments that it's not an issue of cost, but of caring, spending our time rather than our money on those we love most. The gifts inside may not matter, but by replacing limp jokes with daft dares and conversational challenges, crackers like these can bring sparkle and magical mayhem to the Christmas dining table.

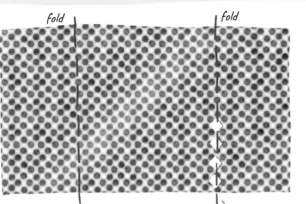

Cut out a 12 x 7in (30 x 18cm) piece of paper (it can be plain, fancy, or triple-layered tissue).

Make two folds 3in/7.5cm in from each end and snip out small triangles all the way along to create perforations.

HOW TO MAKE A CRACKER

Unfold and place right side of paper face down.

Hold a toilet roll tube in place with a smudge of glue, feed through a cracker snap, and secure with tape.

Attach double-sided sticky tape on one long edge.

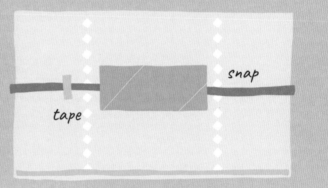

Roll up and stick the long edges together to create a tube, then tie on ribbon around the perforations at one end.

Put a gift, hat, and cracker challenge into the tube, then seal in the contents with the second ribbon tie at the other end.

Add a band of contrasting paper around the center of the cracker and other embellishment as you fancy.

CUSTOMIZE YOUR CRACKERS WITH PERSONALIZED GIFTS AND CHALLENGES *TO ENSURE HILARIOUS TABLE TALK

*Let these examples inspire you to invent your own challenges.

Announce a directive which lasts the whole meal and see who snoozes...(may be repeated as often as desired)

GIFTS

posh sweets · lottery ticket · jewelry or cufflinks · lipstick · subscription · membership · tickets · charity pin badge · key ring · mini perfume or aftershave · temporary tattoo · invitation · tiny toy · dog whistle · practical joke · marriage proposal · voucher · a clue to a present too big for a cracker! · "I promise to..." pledge · chocolate · hair clip · mini pen

go! remove your hat, everyone copies (don't be last!)

go! suddenly freeze, everyone copies (don't be last!)

go! every time you say "Christmas," who can say "ho! ho! ho!" first?

go! start a conversation to the tune of a Christmas carol and everyone carry it on in turn

Nominate any one person to talk on this subject for one whole minute

one a true friend

one my ideal partner

one plans for the rest of my life

one my finest hour!

all if you were granted three wishes by a genie, what would they be?

all how would you spend (a specified sum of money)?

all describe your three best assets

all what one thing would you change about yourself and why?

Complete your secret mission before the end of the meal...

secret say three specified words by the end of the meal without being challenged (e.g. Colombian, vomit)

secret get someone to throw some food!

secret start a controversial conversation and get someone to shout at you in disagreement

secret pay each person around the table a compliment without arousing suspicion

Each person needs a slip of paper and a pencil to write out their secret answers. These are passed to the challenger, who sporadically reads one out. A communal discussion follows about who wrote it (everyone giving nothing away). After two minutes everyone presents their guess and the challenger awards post-meal kitchen duties for all incorrect answers!

ALL THE TRIMMINGS

Sometimes it's the odd special finishing touch that's remembered most, as Mrs Nimble Christmas knows well. At this busy time of year, perhaps we can all benefit from a few of her tricks, which include easy ideas for decoration and food presentation. A few simple finishing flourishes can transform your home and your meals with a minimum of effort and maximum effect.

On Christmas Day Mr JW Christmas rolls his sausagemeat stuffing into little balls and skewers them together to construct mini snowmen, with tiny pieces of raw carrots for their noses. Every year, different visitors are overjoyed by them and declare it the best Christmas meal they've ever had. It probably is, knowing Mr JW, but his sausage snowmen certainly play their part.

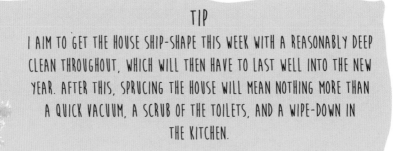

TIP
I AIM TO GET THE HOUSE SHIP-SHAPE THIS WEEK WITH A REASONABLY DEEP CLEAN THROUGHOUT, WHICH WILL THEN HAVE TO LAST WELL INTO THE NEW YEAR. AFTER THIS, SPRUCING THE HOUSE WILL MEAN NOTHING MORE THAN A QUICK VACUUM, A SCRUB OF THE TOILETS, AND A WIPE-DOWN IN THE KITCHEN.

The main cook-ahead task this week is to make some Christmas dinner side dishes (and a vegan or vegetarian option if we need it) and find a space for them in the freezer. How much I get made depends on my available time; I almost always buy in certain elements ready-made. Really good homemade stuffing is a must, along with sharp cranberry sauce and some cook-ahead gravy (which no store-bought offering can possibly match). This week I even parboil the potatoes and then freeze them, so that on Christmas Day they simply go straight into the oven. By freezing everything I can in foil dishes (stackable in the freezer), much is oven-ready on Christmas Day, which frees up the hob and reduces the mammoth kitchen sink session when we should be enjoying the festivities.

SEVEN FINISHING FLOURISHES
IN THE KITCHEN AND AROUND THE HOUSE

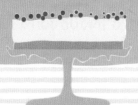

1 A scattering of **herbs** enhances any meal. Buy them growing or keep bunches fresh in the refrigerator by wrapping stems in saturated kitchen paper. Grow rosemary in a pot or in the garden if you can—it's marvellous, not just for cooking, but also for adding to decorations!

2 ***Edible gold leaf*** (placed with tweezers on cakes or desserts in the tiniest quantity), edible dust (to smudge lightly over cookies or chocolates), or sprinkles of edible glitter elevate sweet offerings to luxury level.

3 Melt stubs of old candles in a heatproof jar or foil container, and dip berried stems, leaves, and whole fruits with stalks too—apples, pears, or cherries (or any artificial pieces)—in the wax a couple of times for **classy decorations**.

4 For the **Christmas table**, tie small sprigs of palest honesty or blue-green eucalyptus (you need only buy one stem from the florist) around a napkin with ribbon or raffia, adding a few berries for decoration (waxed or not!).

5 Scatter **finely-chopped nuts** over breakfasts, desserts, salads, and couscous. To make nutty butters to melt over cooked vegetables, mix together 4tbsp/50g softened butter with zest of 1 lemon (or orange), and ⅓ cup/50g chopped toasted hazelnuts or almonds. Roll in waxed (greaseproof) paper and refrigerate, to slice off as required.

6 The exquisite and jewel-like quality of **pomegranate seeds** enhances salads, couscous, and desserts. Iced redcurrants (straight from the freezer) make a beautifully wintery garnish, too.

7 To make **snowy, sparkly table displays** or decorate cakes and cheesecakes, simply beat 1 egg white to a foam, brush onto any small fruit (e.g. figs, cherries, grapes), then dip into or sprinkle on sugar to cover. Leave to dry overnight.

CHRISTMAS DINNER SIDES

SWEET POTATO MASH

For a tiny dollop of vibrant color as much as its delicious taste.

Bake 4 scrubbed sweet potatoes in their skins (pricked a few times) at 400°F/gas mark 6/200°C for 45–50 minutes. Leave to cool a little then scoop out the flesh and mash it together with 1tbsp grated Parmesan, 2tbsp/25g butter, 1 tsp/5ml maple syrup, and a large pinch each of salt and cayenne pepper.

SAUSAGEMEAT STUFFING

Combine 1lb/500g sausagemeat with the zest of 1 unwaxed orange, 1 crushed garlic clove, 1tbsp finely-chopped sage leaves, and ½ cup/50g toasted walnuts, roughly chopped. Form into balls and freeze in a foil tray. Defrost then bake at 350°F/gas mark 4/180°C for 35 minutes, until golden brown.

WHEREVER THERE'S SAUSAGEMEAT, THERE SITS ONE HUNGRY SPANIEL IN OUR HOUSE...

EASY CRANBERRY SAUCE

Put 3 heaped cups/300g fresh cranberries in a saucepan with 2tbsp/30ml port, ½ cup/125g light brown soft sugar, the zest and juice of 1 orange, and a few sprigs of rosemary. Simmer until all berries are burst (about 10 minutes), cool, and freeze. Can be defrosted then reheated in the microwave or on the hob on Christmas Day.

ROAST POTATOES

Parboil peeled potatoes for 7 minutes, drain, and then, with the lid on, shake with a few tbsps of semolina. Cool, open freeze on a tray, then bag up. Defrost and roast in a very hot oven in goose fat as normal. Or skip the freezing bit and simply prepare your potatoes this way on Christmas Eve.

COOK-AHEAD GRAVY

On a roasting tray, place 2 turkey legs, 2 onions, 2 carrots, and 2 sticks of celery (all chopped in half), 3 chopped rashers of streaky bacon, and some bay leaves and finely-chopped rosemary. Drizzle with oil, then roast at 400°F/gas mark 6/200°C for 1 hour. Remove to the hob, strip the meat off the bones, add 3¼ pt/1.5 liters chicken stock, and simmer for 20 minutes. Strain, cool, then freeze.

SPICED RED CABBAGE

In a large casserole gently heat 3½tbsp/50g butter and 1 tbsp/15g light brown soft sugar until dissolved, then add 1 large cooking apple and 1 large onion (both finely chopped). Sweat for about 5 minutes then add 1 red cabbage (finely sliced), 4tbsp/60ml red wine vinegar, 2tbsp/30ml port, 1tsp mixed spice, seasoning, and 2 bay leaves. Simmer gently for 45 minutes, stirring occasionally. Stir in 2 tbsp/30ml redcurrant jelly, then cool. I freeze this in a few separate portions in lidded foil trays. On Christmas Day it can be defrosted, then heated in the oven at 350°F/gas mark 4/180°C for about 30 minutes.

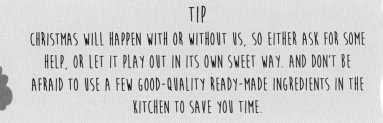

TIP

CHRISTMAS WILL HAPPEN WITH OR WITHOUT US, SO EITHER ASK FOR SOME HELP, OR LET IT PLAY OUT IN ITS OWN SWEET WAY. AND DON'T BE AFRAID TO USE A FEW GOOD-QUALITY READY-MADE INGREDIENTS IN THE KITCHEN TO SAVE YOU TIME.

TIME FOR YOURSELF

So, house and imminent visitors are sorted, food shopping lists and the Christmas dinner are all under control. Now it's our turn for some attention, Mrs Christmas! Hopefully by now, we'll have done much of our rushing around but most likely put our own needs to the bottom of the pile in the process. We may simply feel too overwhelmed by it all, in which case it's time to stop, work out what can be abandoned or delegated, and take a rest.

Before the school break begins, let's block out some time to look after our busy, overstretched selves—whether it's just a hot slow soak in the bath or more elaborate self-care, in anticipation of a few gatherings or parties over the next few weeks. In 1925, beauty "editress" Greta of *Woman's World* magazine advised reader Nancy not to annoy her husband and spoil his Christmas Day by putting rouge on her cheeks—far better to apply a very hot sponge and then slap them morning and night for the whole month of December, to ensure the perfect Christmas complexion. During World War Two, women whose soldier-husbands were expected home for Christmas were encouraged by *Wife and Home* magazine to rub an old silk handkerchief over their hair for a glorious shine and to use peroxide for cigarette stains and obstinate under-nail grubbiness on their work-roughened hands.

We may not worry in quite the same way nowadays, but Mrs RH Christmas still makes her hands a pre-Christmas priority and has a manicure for its glamour factor, even if it's all she gets round to. When things get hectic in the kitchen, she finds that nice nails negate any sense of drudgery. Rather, she's simply Nigella Lawson, playing the glamorous lead on a theatrical stage that just happens to be her kitchen…

STORE-BOUGHT SHORTCUTS

READY-MADE TARTLET CASES

Fill ¾ full with caramelized onion chutney and goat cheese, or fig jam and Dolcelatte, then top up with a mixture of 1 seasoned beaten egg to each 1 tbsp/15ml heavy (double) cream; bake at 350°F/gas mark 4/ 180°C for 10 minutes. For a sweet filling requiring no baking, combine 2 parts mascarpone with 1 part lemon curd and top with a few frozen redcurrants.

FLOURED TORTILLA WRAPS

Make easy quesadillas by placing 1 wrap in a dry frying pan, covering it with grated cheese, some red onion, and de-seeded red chilli (both finely chopped). Place another wrap on top and dry sauté (fry) for 4 minutes, turning over halfway through. Slice up like a pizza. For a sweet filling, try Nutella and mini marshmallows!

SAUCES AND STUFFING

Add a splash of port and some cranberry jelly to ready-made gravy.

Stir in a little apple purée and a large pinch of ground cinnamon to ready-made cranberry sauce.

Throw some chopped cooked chestnuts (vacuum-packed or from a jar) and a large pinch of nutmeg into ready-made stuffing.

GARLIC FLATBREADS

Serve as mini pizzas by spreading (thinly) with caramelized onion chutney, prosciutto, and sliced goat cheese. Alternatively spread on red pepper pesto, a scattering of finely-chopped thyme, and lots of mozzarella. Bake both at 425°F/gas mark 7/ 220°C for 10 minutes.

MINCE PIES

Prize off the pastry lid, dollop in 1tsp mascarpone, and top with grated white marzipan. Replace the lid, then bake at 310°F/gas mark 3–4/170°C for 5 minutes. Serve warm, dusted with confectioners' (icing) sugar.

SHOPPING LISTS

CREATE

NON-FOOD

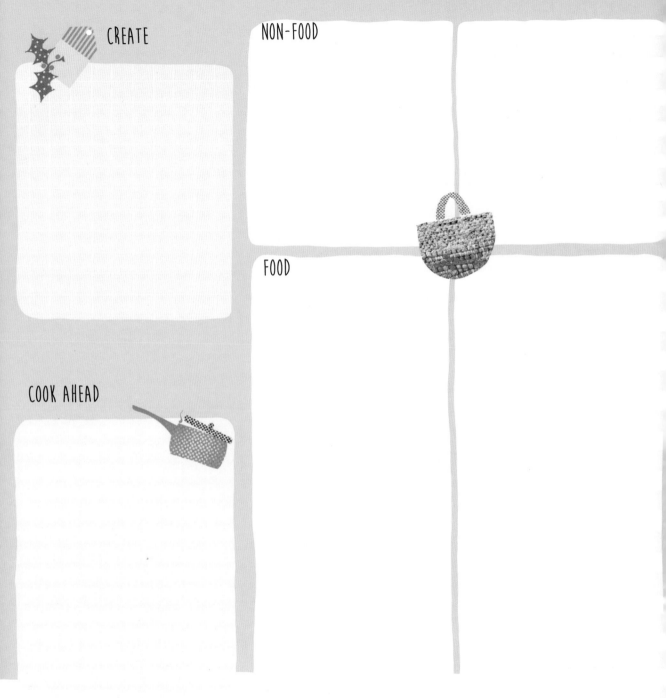

FOOD

COOK AHEAD

THIS WEEK: Check the Christmas tree water level, feed your Christmas cake, and bottle up alcoholic gifts you've made. Why not have a family wrapping session and make a special occasion of it?

EAT

ORGANIZE

MON

TUES

WEDS

THUR

FRI

SAT

SUN

HOST

MID-DECEMBER

CHAPTER 10
WEEK OF CHRISTMAS

"Something homemade is just the Christmas ticket for those we love the most—or indeed for those who have the most!"

TRADITIONS OLD AND NEW

Established traditions are often precious to our vision of Christmas, but that's not to say new rituals and habits we acquire can't command the same affection. I especially love a tradition followed by Mrs EB Christmas, who's fostered countless children over the years. She gives every child she cares for a good chunk of time and undivided attention to help them plan, make, and wrap their presents. Mrs EB always makes her "red soup" (of tomatoes and red bell peppers) for Christmas Eve lunch that her children declare scrumptious, and she reads her little ones "'Twas the Night Before Christmas" before they hang their stockings. That same night Mrs AG Christmas and her family will be huddled around their table-top raclette grill, feasting in alpine style on potatoes, charcuterie, pickles, and vegetables—all smothered in molten cheese. Contemplating this cheery vision, I am pleased to remember that it is never too late to adopt a new tradition.

Mrs SS Christmas and her circle always go carol singing for charity in the local streets (may more of us adopt this lovely custom!). And she couldn't contemplate the season without festive paper towel and toilet paper. Miss LP Christmas hosts a blind tasting of store-bought mince pies for her friends and family. Mrs CH Christmas has special brushed cotton bed linen that goes on the week before Christmas, and a communal Christmas jigsaw puzzle that starts on December 1st for everyone coming and going to complete, right up until Christmas Eve—when fish pie is always on the menu. In Mr JW Christmas' house, it is he who captains the entire Christmas ship and wakes his adult children on Christmas morning with champagne cocktails and festive canapés, delighting in the creativity and surprise of such small-scale offerings. These are then followed by a Christmas morning group selfie in pajamas.

Another Mr Christmas—JM—has since the year dot filmed interviews with his children by the Christmas tree, discussing the year that's just passed and dreams for the one ahead—hilarious and precious festive treasure captured on camera, of which I am highly envious! Mrs JLM Christmas and her family always watch old family videos from Christmases past on Christmas Eve. We have an A1 art folder in which I've put all the children's festive drawings, cards, lists, and letters to Father Christmas over the years—though perhaps it doesn't quite compare to the magic of moving pictures.

FUN AND GAMES

Games and communal activities have always been central to the festive tradition. As Christmas fast approaches, keeping our little ones busy and content seems especially vital. Whenever mine have asked me what I would most like for Christmas, my reply has never varied. "Happy children who do not squabble, please." When they were young, I'd get out a box of playthings we saved especially for Christmas time, including a few festive films, books, and puzzles, and the odd surprise toy for moments when distraction could thwart any rumblings of disharmony. If your children aren't too tiny (or too big), then combine a few friends with a good dressing-up box, for some make-believe improvisation, ballet, plays, and pantomime. Don't forget to have your phone or video camera at the ready, so that you can capture their sweet performance for eternity…

It's worth asking around for games that friends like to play. Charades is always a winner, as is Consequences, a paper and pencil game we've played at Christmas ever since I can remember. And as children, my sisters and I loved another daft game we called Squeak Piggy Squeak (a variation of Blind Man's Buff) which would induce uncontrollable giggling—mostly from my grandmother.

These are simple pleasures and ones our forebears would undoubtedly have recognized. The activities of Victorian families were well described in children's annuals of the time. They danced away Christmas Eve in their parlor, and played Hunt the Slipper, Forfeits, Romps, and Snapdragon, a somewhat precarious game which involved grabbing raisins from a burning bowl set alight with alcohol.

Without the modern trappings of technology and media, our ancestors devised their own merry entertainment which was all they could have wished for—because stopping to play and interact with each other is nothing short of a treat. We can learn from that; a bit of belly laughter surely has to be worth turning our phones and the TV off occasionally in the special days ahead.

And if not a game, how about a communal crafting activity? Mrs SG Christmas once propped up a big envelope in each place at her Christmas dinner table. Inside were materials for making an improvised paper hat, to be completed within a set time, while the turkey was being carved.

A WARM WELCOME

Seeing our home all ready and bountiful for special family times makes me thankful. If I am on top of everything, I always think now is the perfect time for a bit of spontaneity, inviting local friends over, even if it's just for a cup of tea with a slice of gingerbread cake. Mrs Humbug Christmas, please take note—keeping things simple cuts down on the stress, the preparation, and the clearing up, so there's no reason not to make merry with those we love.

It's for these local friends, as well as family we'll be seeing in the coming days, that I like to make some small edible gifts. My children always wanted to join in with this happy task when they were small, so over the years I have gathered a few very simple recipes together, which everyone (with clean hands!) can help to make. They all make special presents, particularly for those in our children's world who make a big difference but can sometimes get overlooked: teaching assistants, school bus drivers, and cafeteria staff.

Something homemade is just the ticket for those we love the most, or indeed those who already have the most. I generally choose just one or two recipes each year and make enough for multiple gifts—with a little thought about their presentation too, so that the container or wrapping is part of its joy. Last year Miss KD Christmas gave us a "walking in" gift of homemade cranberry gin, which was made even more charming by her decanting it into the prettiest glass-stoppered bottle.

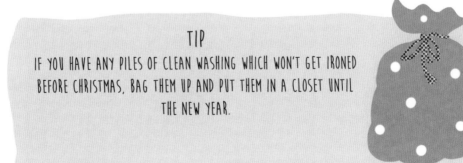

TIP
IF YOU HAVE ANY PILES OF CLEAN WASHING WHICH WON'T GET IRONED BEFORE CHRISTMAS, BAG THEM UP AND PUT THEM IN A CLOSET UNTIL THE NEW YEAR.

EDIBLE GIFTS

EACH RECIPE MAKES 3 OR 4 LOVELY PRESENTS.

CHOCOLATE CANDIED PEEL

Cut ½-in/1-cm wide strips of peel from 4 unwaxed oranges after removing pith as necessary to make them approximately ¼in/0.5cm thick. Place the strips in a large saucepan with 1pt/500ml water, bring to a boil, and simmer for 1 hour, adding 2 cups/400g white sugar halfway through. Lift the peel out with a slotted spoon onto a lined baking sheet and cook in the oven at 250°F/gas mark ½/130°C for 40 minutes. While still hot, toss the strips in white sugar then leave to cool. Melt 3½oz/100g chocolate and dip one end of each strip in it, then leave to set.

TIPSY TRUFFLES

In a food processor, blend 10½oz/300g lightly crushed Oreo cookies, ⅔ cup/150g cream cheese, and 1tbsp/15ml liqueur.* Roll the mixture into 1-in/2.5-cm balls and freeze for 20 minutes on waxed (greaseproof) paper on a baking sheet. Dip the truffles in two kinds of melted chocolate (5oz/150g of each), top with cookie crumbs or other festive sprinkles, and leave to cool.

*e.g. Baileys, Disarrono, Whiskey, or Brandy—or for a nonalcoholic version, add orange juice.

BRANDY BUTTER

Cream together 2 sticks + 1tbsp/ 250g softened butter and 1¼ cups/250g superfine (caster) sugar until light and fluffy. Beat in the zest of 1 lemon and 5tbsp/75ml brandy. Spoon the butter out onto a 20-in/ 50-cm length of waxed (greaseproof) paper, then use the edges to roll it into a 12-in/30-cm long sausage. Refrigerate, then, when hard, cut into three pieces and wrap each one in waxed paper, festive twine, and a label—to be kept in the refrigerator for melting on Christmas pudding (see page 61) or mince pies (see page 105).

For savory gifts, why not make
a few jars of Fig Relish (page 37)
or some Spiced Nuts (page 42)?

PECAN PUDDINGS
Makes about 30

In a food processor, roughly chop 2¼ cups/200g pecan nuts. Add
20 pitted dates and ½tsp sea salt, then blend. Form the mixture into
1-in/2.5-cm balls and refrigerate. Decorate with melted white chocolate as
"custard" and a sliver of pistachio as a leaf in the top, or simply roll in
confectioners' (icing) sugar for a vegan alternative.

MRS LSM CHRISTMAS' RAW CHOCOLATE GINGERS
Makes 3 little gifts

Melt 1 cup/110g cacao butter in a bain marie over a low
heat. Whisk in 1 cup/90g cacao powder and 3tbsp/45ml maple
or agave syrup until very smooth. Pour the mixture into silicon
chocolate molds with a piece of crystalized ginger in the bottom
(or dried cranberry or cherry if preferred) and refrigerate for
an hour before turning out.

I make mini "trees" from this
mixture in cone-shaped molds,
adding a touch of edible gold at
the top for the star after I've
turned them out.

THE ICING ON THE CAKE

In the kitchen, putting the marzipan on our Christmas cake is on my to-do list this week. Mrs Nimble Christmas simply buys a good-quality white marzipan—though making it ourselves really isn't tricky and is streets ahead of anything store-bought, so my tastebuds tell me. But then they were spoilt rotten by my very kind grandmother, who always made a huge homemade loaf of marzipan for us as children, both to much on rather indulgently and to shape into a medley of exotic fruits or blobby figures to top our Christmas cake—far more versatile and tasty than Plasticine!

Once your marzipan has been left to dry for a day or two, it's time to ice the Christmas cake. There are all kinds of simple ideas in magazines and on websites like Pinterest if you'd prefer something more sophisticated than my suggestions opposite, and it need not be the serious affair it was back in 1969. Back then, an article in *The Lady* magazine declared that icing the cake was every cook's moment to shine. And clearly not for resorting to what is my own habitual approach—swirling on icing "snow" and plonking some ready-made decorations on top!

TIP
A DAY OR TWO BEFORE CHRISTMAS EVE, FREE UP SOME SPACE IN THE REFRIGERATOR FOR FRESH GROCERIES, MOVING ANYTHING THAT JUST NEEDS TO BE KEPT COOL (RATHER THAN COLD) INTO A WELL-SEALED BOX OR BAG. THIS CAN BE KEPT OUTSIDE IF IT'S NOT FROSTY, OR IN A GARAGE OR SHED IF IT IS.

DECORATING THE CHRISTMAS CAKE

SEE PAGE 63 FOR A CHRISTMAS CAKE RECIPE.

MINI FESTIVE FOREST

Make some trees to go on top!

Cut 3-in/7.5-cm pieces from the ends of fir branches and pull off 1in/2.5cm of needles from the cut end to create a trunk. Wrap the trunk in plastic wrap. Stick a star cut from orange peel or foil paper to the top of each tree, and insert most of the wrapped trunk in the icing. Once all trees are in place, dust with confectioners' (icing) sugar.

MARZIPAN
(for an 8-in/20-cm cake)

Sift 1¾ cups/250g confectioners' (icing) sugar into a mixing bowl, and add 5 cups/500g ground almonds. Mix in a large beaten egg, the zest of an orange, and 1tsp or so of its juice to form a dough. Spread a little confectioners' (icing) sugar on a board and roll out the marzipan to a circle large enough to cover the whole cake. Brush melted and sieved apricot jam all over the cake, then cover it with the rolled-out marzipan, pressing it into the sides.
Trim the edges.

AFTER COVERING THE CAKE, LEAVE THE MARZIPAN TO DRY FOR AT LEAST 24 HOURS BEFORE ICING IT.

ROUGH ROYAL ICING
(for an 8-in/20-cm cake)

Beat 3 egg whites with a whisk until frothy, gradually sifting in 3½ cups/500g confectioners' (icing) sugar until it's all incorporated. Continue beating until the icing forms stiff peaks, then add in 1tsp lemon juice, 1 drop of blue food coloring, and 1tsp glycerine. Spread the icing roughly over the marzipanned cake, to look like snow, then add any decorations. Once the icing is dry, store the cake in an airtight container.

LAST-MINUTE TASKS

However organized we have been so far, there are still a fair few jobs that need finishing off this week. I count my blessings I am not Mrs Christmas a century ago, with a final to-do list as long as her arm: scrubbing wooden draining boards with baking soda solution, then massaging in petroleum jelly for protection against water; starching Christmas linens, or removing smoke stains from all the ivory around the house!

Instead, Mrs AS Christmas finds time to construct any toys and put batteries in place, so that surprises can be hidden under blankets in the shed or loft, safe in the knowledge that arguing over assembly instructions will not be a feature of her family's Christmas Day. Mr JH Christmas likes to plan the wines to be drunk in the days ahead, so they are all in the right place, at the right temperature, at the right moment. It's a serious task, not to be forgotten if his family's Christmas is to be mellow!

Nigella Lawson's best tip (she has many) is deemed by several Mrs Christmases to be the easy but elaborate brining of the turkey over the next few days, which she describes with fabulously festive detail. I'm planning to try it one day.

In the meantime and back to practicalities, I'm mindful that there is still a late cluster of jobs to tick off this close to Christmas. Around December 21st or 22nd, my to-do list can suddenly seem longer than ever, so I find it helpful to have a final three-day planner to help clear my head. It always ends up with scribbles and ticks transferred across from one day to another, but at least it gathers together all my thoughts.

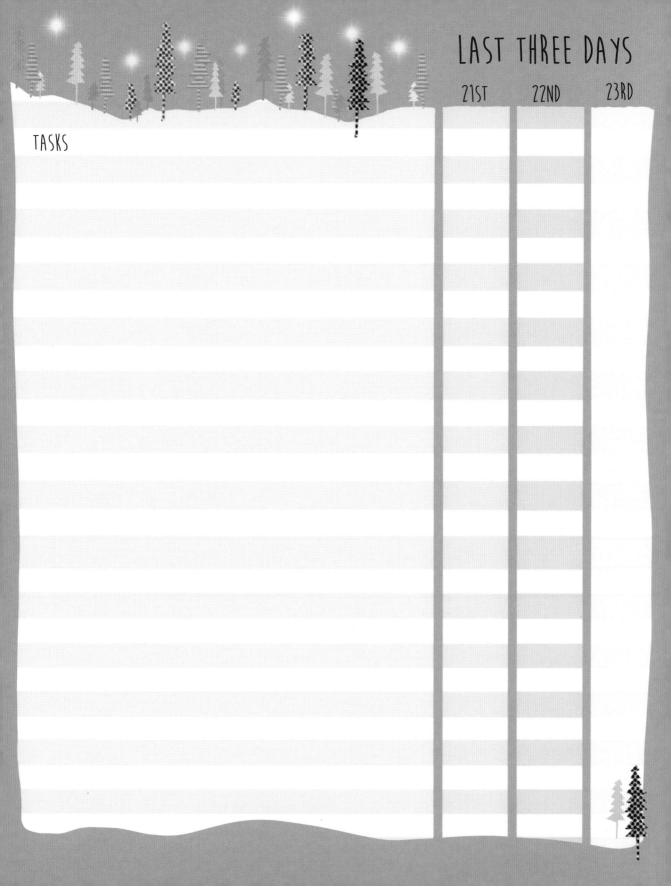

LAST THREE DAYS

TASKS	21ST	22ND	23RD

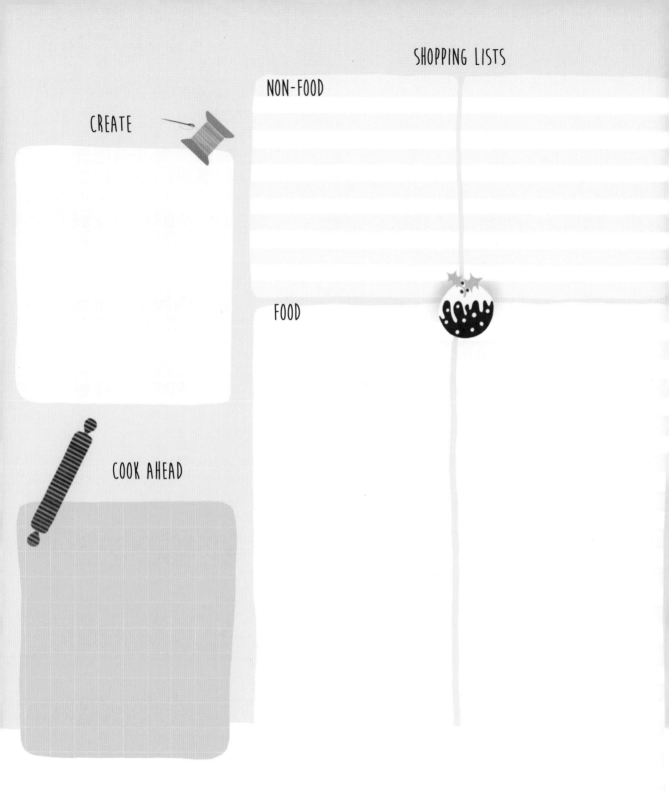

SHOPPING LISTS

NON-FOOD

FOOD

CREATE

COOK AHEAD

THIS WEEK: *Check the Christmas tree water level, mark up the TV guide or make a list of programs/films to watch, sharpen kitchen knives, and start making extra ice.*

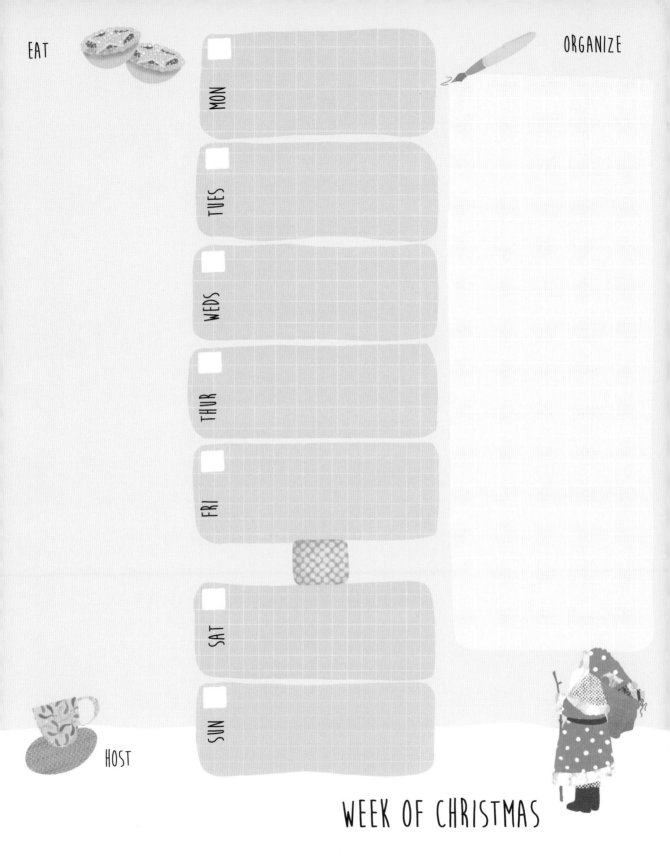

EAT

ORGANIZE

MON

TUES

WEDS

THUR

FRI

SAT

SUN

HOST

WEEK OF CHRISTMAS

CHAPTER 11

CHRISTMAS EVE AND CHRISTMAS DAY

"Making Christmas Eve a day of easygoing communal preparation and relaxation will make a world of difference to the enjoyment of the coming days."

CHRISTMAS EVE

You may feel the need to devise a December 24th mother of all to-do lists, but if the last few months have been filled with plans and preparations, and work patterns permit, don't we deserve to take this special day at a leisurely pace? Making it a day of easygoing communal preparation and relaxation will make a world of difference to our enjoyment in the coming days.

In Germany, as in many other European countries, Christmas Eve is the main day of celebration. Families dress up in their festive best and wait for the big reveal of the decorated tree in their living rooms, after the *Christkind* (Christ child) has been to deliver presents. Mrs KS Christmas near Cologne, Germany is at her busiest on this day, preparing a big meal and presenting *bunter Teller*—decorated plates full of homemade *Plätzchen* (see page 91 for some recipes), along with other sweet treats, nuts, and tangerines, all set out on the Christmas table alongside presents. At her family gathering, carol singing with musical accompaniment is followed by a special evening feast of roast goose with spicy red cabbage and dumplings.

In our home, we do our best to make sure Christmas Eve revolves around time together. I like to get up early, light candles, and lay the Christmas table, complete with a Christmas Eve present at each place. There might be a new board game (only if I can find a brilliant one) or Christmas pajamas, sweaters, or underwear for everyone. When our children were small, we usually gave them something to do or make, which we would help them with during the day.

A highlight for them—even now—is the ceremony of bringing down our stockings from the attic, along with a toddler-sized wooden sleigh for each of our children, which I painted for them when they were babies. The inspiration for these stemmed from the 1960s when my sisters and I were given sturdy Mary Quant-style cardboard boxes in which to store our opened Christmas presents. Our living room stayed tidy, and we all adored having our own treasure boxes in which to organize and rearrange our new toys and protect them from inquisitive sisters. Thirty years later, three little sleighs emerged for my own small children, who would squeal with delight to sit in them and be pushed around the place at top speed. They're a little bashed up now (the sleighs), but otherwise intact and now fiercely defended by the children against any suggestion they've outgrown them. And on Christmas Day, their chaos-containing function certainly still kicks in.

ALL IS CALM

On Christmas Eve we play lots of games and eat far too much, so at some point a big calorie-burning dog walk for our spaniel is a must. Early in the day, we take an hour or so to get a few things done in the kitchen, where our favorite Christmassy choral music plays in the background. Usually everyone is gathered there too, so nothing feels a chore. The only essentials are to defrost any food in the freezer that we'll need for tomorrow, and to make the Bûche de Noel—the sweet-chestnut-filled chocolate yule log we always eat this special night, its taste as Christmassy to us as anything. For Mrs SH Christmas' family in California, her festive apple pie is the treasured equivalent. Mrs BH Christmas back in chilly Britain sorts out tomorrow's vegetables. With a little preparation today, sprouts can be sautéed tomorrow in a jiffy. She throws them into salted boiling water for five minutes, then plunges them into a bowl of cold water (with some ice cubes) to blanch them. They can be drained and stored in the fridge until tomorrow; for roasted carrots and parsnips, they need just one minute in boiling water before being blanched and stored in the same way. Mrs PW Christmas actually cooks her turkey today, then keeps it well covered and cold until Christmas Day. She enthuses that it's perfectly juicy, far easier to carve, and means there's plenty of room in the oven the next day for everything else—and in fact no one's even aware of her strategic trick by the time the turkey's served up on warm plates with piping hot gravy!

CHRISTMAS EVE NOTES

KITCHEN

GENERAL

'TWAS THE NIGHT BEFORE CHRISTMAS

On Christmas Eve, Mr JB Christmas always prepares our evening meal of either baked gammon or a rib of beef on the bone, both providing us with lots of leftover cold cuts for the days after Christmas. After dinner, the main event is writing our letters to Father Christmas, which we'll read aloud before "posting" them up the chimney. It's a sweet exercise if you have little ones—try capturing their words on film as they read out their letters and precious thoughts. Mrs ML Christmas, who has no fireplace, keeps a specially decorated pot for letters to Father Christmas, which sits next to the edibles left out for him, so there's no danger they'll be missed.

Last of all we hang up our stockings, put out brandy and a mince pie for Father Christmas and some carrots for his reindeer, and then the children trot off contentedly to bed. Even now, when my "baby" boy is huge and hairy, all three climb the stairs by candlelight and sleep in the same room just for this magical night. I still feel the frisson of the Christmas Eve bedtime routine, just as I did when my sisters and I tumbled into bed in our best nighties, desperate to stay awake and be asleep at the same time—because, as we all know, Father Christmas only comes to sleeping children.

Once they are tucked up in bed, I lay and rearrange our dining table with its surprise Christmas Day makeover, all ready for breakfast in the morning. After that, assisting Father Christmas on Christmas Eve is Mrs C's delightful privilege—and swift, as long as all has been well prepared in advance, with everything sorted into personalized bags, the contents of stocking toes separated out and at the ready. Mrs SH Christmas in California only places her family's presents under the tree once all her children are in bed, to add a dash of excitement to the following morning, even though they are now all grown-ups.

Collapsing into bed on Christmas Eve night is bliss in a nutshell—done, dusted, yet all to come… Not that the best laid plans always work out—a few glasses of deepest red wine and some last-minute wrapping is a perfectly joyful alternative to the Christmas Eve routine I describe, as Mrs BW Christmas will verify. She knows, though, to make sure bedtime isn't too late, as bumping into Father Christmas is a no-no.

A CENTERPIECE

A line of small vases filled with either winter blooms or greenery will last well. Floating candles in a shallow bowl look pretty, too, or a sparkly feather boa snaking its way down the center of the table—just mind the gravy!

I generally prefer to hang a display above the table, so there's more space for everything else on it. This could be a candelabra or an interestingly-shaped branch adorned with baubles, pine cones, greenery, and small, battery-powered lights for a magical touch. I leave a small white hook in the ceiling all year round to hang this from.

PLACE NAMES

Making place cards can be a cheery task for children to get stuck into—with pens, glue, and glitter. Help them fold thin card in half, then cut out a shape through both halves, keeping the crease intact at the top so that it will stand up. Trees, crowns, and bells look sweet with embellishments stuck on. For a natural look, wind lengths of ivy around a napkin and write a name on one of the leaves in a metallic or white paint pen. Or cut leaf shapes from colored card and punch a hole in one end, to slide over the stalk of a rosy red apple or a crisp green pear.

THE TABLECLOTH

Like me, you may have favorite tablecloths or runners you keep specially for Christmas Day and beyond. If not, you can't go wrong with a crisp white cloth, which can be dressed up in all sorts of ways.

CHRISTMAS MORNING

An unnamed grandmother of early Victorian days, whose heartening example deserves to be celebrated, put warm hospitality and generosity at the very heart of Christmas Day, when according to one appreciative guest her house "was filled to overflowing." Amid the "noise and the mirth," she always provided a generous feast. "The goose, the huge joints of beef, and most of all the plum puddings and mince-pies disappeared … with surprising celerity. The home-brewed beer and home-made wines were done equal justice to; to say nothing of bread and butter, plum-cake and muffins which followed."

First thing on Christmas morning, we Mrs Christmases should, recommended *Good Housekeeping* magazine back in 1944, find a peaceful hour to sort out our hair, face, and hands. The success of all our efforts would, after all, mean so little if our hair were wispy, our complexions dull, or we felt compelled to sit on our shabby hands. Mrs CB Christmas does at least keep hand cream and her lipstick handy in her kitchen on these special days, though talented cook Mrs KN Christmas would have failed miserably by that 1940s' measure. The moment she awakes on Christmas morning, she brings her turkey to room temperature and parboils her potatoes ready for roasting. My own attentions are not much focused on my appearance either, as countless early morning Christmas Day photos of me with mascara smudges and birds' nest hair will testify. I always wake up early, thinking of my beloved grandmother making her way downstairs to light her Christmas Day fire by candlelight.

I wait patiently—and joyfully—for the hour to arrive that's civilized enough to wake the house with the chiming of an old bell I keep especially for the occasion. Everyone waits upstairs, while I make tea. Mr JB Christmas lights the fire and candles in the living room, and puts a crackly old vinyl of Nat King Cole singing his "Christmas Song" on the record player—this tune has accompanied the opening of my stocking for every Christmas morning I can ever remember. Only to Nat's smooth, dreamy tones are we allowed to rush in, to see if Father Christmas has blessed us with his kind presence again this year.

ALL IS BRIGHT

Later on Christmas morning, after eating a special breakfast, going to church, and getting outside for some fresh air, we start thinking about lunch. Mrs AS Christmas doesn't feel overburdened with kitchen tasks on this day, as she makes and freezes much of her Christmas meal ahead of time, so it is no more effort than a normal roast meal. She eases any pressure by interspersing each course with games, presents, walks, or films, so that the whole meal lasts well into the evening.

There is plenty of advice out there on what to do and when for your Christmas meal, and what I find most helpful is having a timetable (ideally written out well ahead of the day) of all the different elements, starting with when we want to eat, then working backward. That list is handy to keep for the following year, because what we serve rarely changes! It also, in theory, prevents anything being forgotten, particularly the Christmas pudding, which we like to eat on our laps watching the Queen's Christmas speech in front of the fire. It's there we open our presents, having abided by an ancient family rule—Waiting for Lunch to Go Down—once the gloomiest prospect imaginable to my little, beyond-excited self. Yet so embedded is it in our Christmas tradition, that I've somehow passed it on to my own children. When the well-negotiated nine minutes is up, one of us becomes "present fairy" and hands out presents from our special sack which sits under the tree. We jot down the contents as we open them to ease the process of recall later in the day when we speak to loved ones on the phone, or write to thank others in the New Year. After games galore in front of the fire (and occasionally the odd snore on the sofa), we might nip into the kitchen to put together a cheese board or a platter of goodies for a late evening feast.

THE BIG FESTIVE MEAL

TIME	TASK

Remember that a cooked turkey can sit wrapped (tightly) in foil and covered by a dishcloth (teatowel) or two for a couple of hours, freeing up oven space for everything else.

CHRISTMAS DAY NOTES

USE THIS PAGE TO WRITE DOWN ANYTHING YOU NEED TO REMEMBER TO DO ON CHRISTMAS DAY. I ALWAYS KEEP MY OWN NOTES FROM LAST YEAR AS AN AIDE-MEMOIRE.

TO EAT AROUND 1.30 PM

Time	Task
9.45 am	turkey crown out of fridge
10.30 am	take roast potatoes out of freezer
10.45 am	turkey in oven
11.30 am	lay table, bring wine to room temperature, white wines into fridge
12.25 pm	turkey out, cover and rest, turn up oven, goose fat for potatoes in oven
12.35 pm	potatoes in oven
12.45 pm	sausage meat/pigs in blankets in oven
12.50 pm	blanched carrots/parsnips in oven, red cabbage (covered) in oven
1.00 pm	pudding on to steam
1.10 pm	reheat gravy (add turkey juices), put plates/serving dishes in warming oven
1.15 pm	sauté sprouts/pancetta SERVE CANAPÉS
1.20 pm	carve turkey/keep covered
1.25 pm	heat bread sauce, keep warm in dish, put cranberry sauce in dish
1.30 pm	wine/water on table plates out of oven and serve, move pudding to simmering oven
2.55 pm	warm brandy for pudding
3.00 pm	serve pudding with clotted cream and brandy

Breakfast—scrambled eggs, salmon, dill

Replace champagne in fridge

Christmas collar Barney

Phone Aunties M and C, Rev P, and RM

Pudding!

Teatime—decorate trifle, bring in cheeses, remember cake, sloe gin

Defrost croissants for tomorrow

Top up drinks—refrigerator

Logs

Christmas hot water bottles

PRESENTS RECEIVED

RECIPIENT

SENDER	GIFT	THANKS

RECIPIENT

SENDER	GIFT	THANKS

RECIPIENT

SENDER	GIFT	THANKS

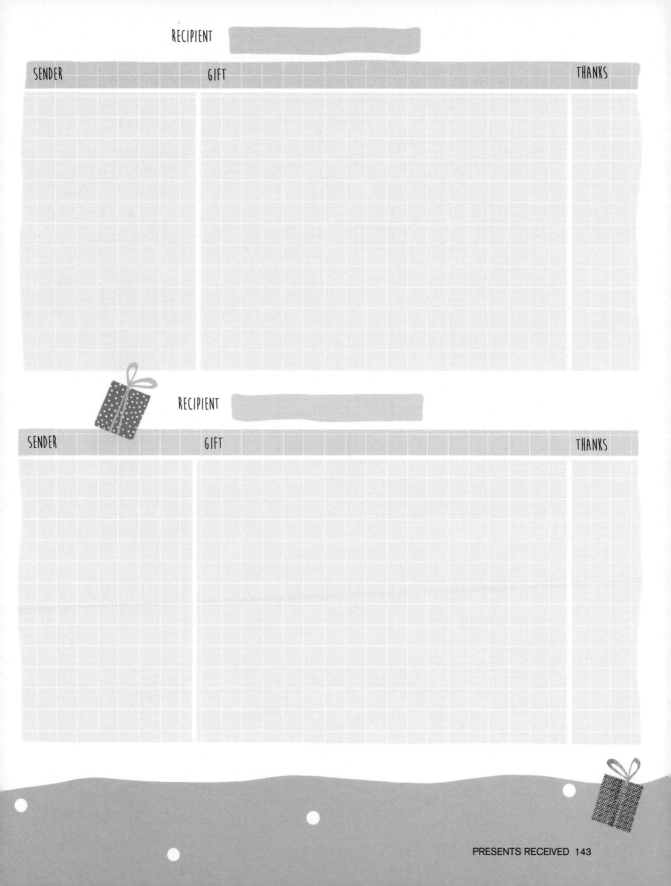

RECIPIENT

SENDER	GIFT	THANKS

CHAPTER 12

WEEK OF NEW YEAR AND JANUARY

"The value of spending time with our loved ones, in our places of sanctuary ... is probably greater than it's ever been."

TWELVE DAYS OF CHRISTMAS

In many ways, December 26th—St Stephen's Day, or Boxing Day as it is known in the UK—and the few days beyond it are sublime. If we like, we can wallow in relaxation as the world momentarily winds down. In our house, we keep the fire lit all day, read the books we have been given, pamper ourselves with new products we have received, play games, and watch movies together. If we have shopped well before Christmas, there will be everything we need in store to eat like kings for many days to come, with minimal cooking to be done. Mrs RH Christmas delves into her "in-house deli" with joy.

If you're lucky, this week's planner will have plenty of blank spaces for doing nothing much, but the welcome change of gear can be interspersed with a little spontaneous socializing, to eke out the festive feeling a little bit longer and boost our moods if we are feeling a little flat. We sometimes visit famly we've not been able to see at Christmas time, or invite family friends who live far away to come and stay before the arrival of the new year. Mrs AM Christmas arranges an evening of board games and leftovers, or a film night where all the festive chocolates and other treats can be consumed before new-year resolutions begin.

TIP
TAKE A LEAF FROM THE BOOK OF GENERATIONS PAST AND EXTEND YOUR CELEBRATIONS ALL THROUGH EPIPHANY TO JANUARY 6TH. PLAN A FEW ACTIVITIES AT HOME THAT EVERYONE CAN JOIN IN WITH.

REFLECTIONS

Reflecting on Christmas while it is still fresh in our minds is a useful exercise, especially if we record our thoughts. I've written countless notes to myself through the years. Never buy one little daughter a pair of sparkly socks and not the other. Don't run out of tea lights or lemons. Buy fewer but more fabulous cheeses. Get to Midnight Mass in plenty of time. Agree a digital detox again. Remember carpet stain remover. Ask myself more regularly, "Can this wait until the new year?"

Having sweated the detail, we can ponder with family and friends the bigger picture, too. What makes Christmas most special for each of us? By brainstorming and documenting our combined conclusions, perhaps using the next two pages as a basis for discussion, we can create our own heartfelt festive blueprint which will be valuable when we begin our preparations all over again next year!

So before our focus switches to new-year celebrations, get out the notebooks and pens and gather everyone up. Over this next week, do involve the children too, as you talk about celebrating Christmas well. Counting our blessings is something we could all probably do with practicing more often! Then, with gratitude and optimism, we may begin our New Year's preparations. Some years, I confess, I'm happy to skip anything too organized on December 31st; other years, it's fun to go to town and plan some party fun.

TIP
CHRISTMAS CAN BE EVEN MORE ENRICHING WHEN WE ENHANCE THE BEST-LOVED ELEMENTS AND DROP THE ONES THAT, IN TRUTH, BRING LITTLE REAL JOY.

Write your names here, then everyone can rank the
following in order of importance at Christmas time
(from 1—most important to 10—least important).

CHRISTMAS CONFESSIONS

Charity and kindness

Sustainability

Creativity

Worship/spirituality

Relaxation

Socializing

Food and drink

Presents and/or stockings

Games and communal activities

Events and entertainment

(or substitute different categories of your own)

GENERAL NOTES

CHRISTMAS UNWRAPPED

List different aspects of Christmas in your home and ask everyone to place a tick beneath the evaluation they choose (perhaps in different-colored pens). Use the answers as the basis of a kind and compromising discussion about the shape of Christmas in the future.

PERFECT

VERY GOOD

AVERAGE/TOLERABLE

TO BE AMENDED/ SCALED BACK

TO BE AXED!

PRE-CHRISTMAS

CHRISTMAS

POST-CHRISTMAS

LUCKY NEW YEAR

Traditionally, at midnight on New Year's Eve, we kiss those we want to keep on kissing during the coming year; we make sure our larders and purses are full, to ensure future prosperity; and even if we're not warding off evil spirits as our ancestors might have done, we all generally like to make lots of merry noise, whether that's with church bells, fireworks, or—if we're lucky— a jolly good party. If you decide to open your house this year, don't forget to check out all the party planning tips back on pages 40–41—and, in true Scottish form, invite a tall and good-looking stranger into your home just as the clock strikes twelve!

GO SPARKLY, WITH YOUR HOME DECORATIONS, PARTY OUTFIT, AND DRINKS!

SET UP A CHAMPAGNE COCKTAIL BAR WITH DIFFERENT LIQUEURS, A FEW MIXERS (E.G. ELDERFLOWER CORDIAL, GINGER ALE, AND ORANGE JUICE) AND SOME FINISHING TOUCHES (E.G. POMEGRANATE SEEDS, ROSEMARY SPRIGS, AND FRUIT SLICES)

REMEMBER PARTY POPPERS, FAIRY LIGHTS, CANDLES, AND CURLS OF RIBBON STREWN AROUND THE PLACE TO SET THE PARTY SCENE!

AFTER SIMPLE SAVORY NIBBLES (SEE PAGES 42–43 FOR A FEW IDEAS), ARRANGE A SWEET MIDNIGHT FEAST OF CAKES AND ICE CREAM TOPPED WITH SPARKLERS TO WELCOME IN THE NEW YEAR!

DELEGATE FRIENDS TO ORGANIZE A FEW PARTY GAMES AND CREATE SOME NEW YEAR'S PARTY PLAYLISTS— AND OTHERS TO BE IN CHARGE OF BREAKFAST THE NEXT MORNING!

SHOPPING LISTS

NON-FOOD

FOOD

NOTES

THIS WEEK: *This is a good week for a theater or pantomime trip. Why not hold back a few presents for children (and even ourselves) to open after Christmas, so we can all savor each one more slowly?*

 EAT

 ORGANIZE

MON

TUES

WEDS

THUR

FRI

SAT

SUN

HOST

WEEK OF NEW YEAR

JOBS FOR JANUARY

Mrs CS Christmas loves to see her Christmas decks cleared very early in the new year, packing everything away in labeled categories, such as "kitchen windowsill" or "staircase"—particularly useful, she says, when it comes to different strings of lights, which are easily muddled. She removes any batteries and replaces dud bulbs, before winding them up to prevent tangles, all ready for next December. My own Christmas spirits wane more gradually. Clearing away all the decorations always feels incongruous with what is happening outside the windows here in the UK—a dormant and deeply wintery month of January spells hibernation more than any other time of the year for me, so I don't want to make our indoor spaces feel too bleak. Renewal and resolution of any kind can wait just a bit longer!

Candlemas, on February 2nd, marks the end of Epiphany and, for those of us in the northern hemisphere, seems a much better point at which to ease out of our seasonal cocoons. Keeping cozy with throws, blankets, and other wintery comforts is more vital than ever. At the risk of repetition, so too are the candles, with their extraordinary power (in combination with cups of tea and leftover Christmas cake) to lift a gray January afternoon.

A gentle January is nothing short of helpful, because without too much going on, I can usually find time to complete tasks I'd either had to abandon before Christmas, or never got round to starting. An early task is gathering all our Christmas cards and turning the suitable ones into labels for next year. I either cut them by hand or use a heavy-duty label punch. A mini guillotine or scalloped shears are useful too, along with a smaller than standard hole punch for a smarter finish.

TIP
ALTHOUGH I TAKE DOWN MOST OF THE DECORATIONS BY JANUARY 6TH, THOSE WHICH I CAN GET AWAY WITH DESCRIBING AS SEASONAL, RATHER THAN JUST FESTIVE, CAN STAY UP FOR A FEW WEEKS MORE.

Now is also the time for sorting out any used wrapping paper saved from Christmas Day. Lovely tissue paper can be smoothed flat, re-ironed on the coolest setting, wound around an empty wrapping paper tube and held in place with a narrow band of used paper fixed with tape. Pieces of smart wrapping paper—no matter how small—can be trimmed down (cutting away tears, folds, or sellotape marks) and ironed like the tissue paper—on its wrong side to prevent discoloration. Even the pieces that are too marked or creased for reuse can be shredded as filler for present bags. Like Mrs PW Christmas, I might then supplement my wrapping supplies (and cards) by buying wisely in the January sales.

One of my favorite paper crafts is making 3D festive shapes which are quick to create (see pages 154–155), and can be used individually as embellishments for presents or strung together to make garlands. Why not combine making a few of these and having a card recycling session with a few friends in January? It's a great way of catching up on one another's Christmases and creating a little stash of goodies all ready for the next... though if any of the paper you have isn't specifically festive, then your 3D shapes can be anything you like—they are useful for tying on to birthday presents or turning into greetings cards for other occasions during the year.

TIP
CHAPTERS 1 AND 5 COVER MORE WAYS OF USING EITHER OLD
WRAPPING PAPER, OR TINY BITS OF NEW.

3D STARS

Make yourself a thick card template of one equal-sided triangle. On another piece of card, draw around it and reposition it repeatedly to end up with the shape shown here (or trace over this one if you are happy with the size.) Place the template on patterned paper and draw round it with a pencil. Repeat on the same or a contrasting paper, then cut the two shapes out. With the paper patterned side up, make creases along the dotted lines, so that the pink creases fold upward and the green ones the other way (this enables the centers at C to protrude outward more easily when you come to glue the stars together). Next, put one star on top of the other, wrong sides touching, with their A and B positions opposite each other. Then start to glue the five points of each star together, closing the A/B gaps as you do, so that a 3D star is born! Once dry, trim off any excess of paper and punch a hole in one point for hanging, attaching to a gift, or creating a garland with multiple stars.

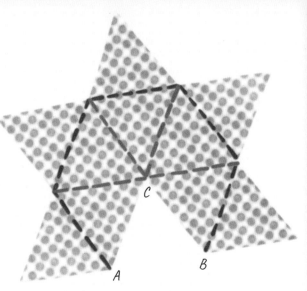

SCRAPS OF WRAP

PYRAMID POUCHES

PERFECT FOR HIDING SMALL TREATS OR FORFEITS, OR TO HANG ON THE TREE.

write message here

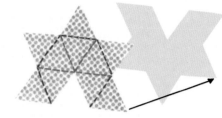

Cut out two rectangles (of equal length) in contrasting papers, making B 1in/2.5cm narrower than A. Glue together the short ends of A to create a tube.

Cover the whole of the reverse side of B in glue, then wrap it around A, with equal borders of A down each side.

When dry, glue the tube together at one end, using a bulldog clip to hold it until dry. Then fill the pouch, press together the open end in the opposite direction—finger on C and thumb on D—and glue together in same way. When dry, punch a hole in one flat edge and hang.

1 Place 3 or 4 pieces of wrapping paper (the same or contrasting) on top of each other, fractionally bigger than the shape you'd like to create.

2 On your sewing machine, using a sturdy needle and the largest stitch size, sew a (roughly) central line down the middle, leaving long tails of thread at each end.

3 Fold in half on the stitch line and cut out half your chosen shape (anything symmetrical, like a bell, tree, or bauble) through all the layers of paper.

4 Open up, fan out the layers, tie to a ribbon or trim the bottom thread, and hang from the top.

String a whole bunch of these together to make a garland, perhaps mixing and matching shapes.

Make small versions to use as gift tags, writing on one leaf of the paper.

Scale them up to make giant decorations.

MAKING MINCEMEAT
A PERFECT TASK FOR JANUARY IN MY BOOK!

MINCEMEAT
(Makes 2 x 1lb/400g jars)

In a large mixing bowl, stir together 2tbsp/30ml each of suet, brandy, and stem ginger syrup with 2½ cups/350g mixed dried fruit and nuts (raisins, sultanas, currants, mixed peel, chopped almonds, chopped dried figs, and chopped glacé cherries). Add 1 grated apple, the zest and a good squeeze of the juice of 1 lemon, 1 cup/200g dark muscovado sugar, 1tsp mixed spice, and 2 finely-chopped knobs of stem ginger. Put into sterilized jars* and keep in a cool, dark place.

*You can sterilize clean dry jars by placing them in an oven at 350°F/gas mark 4/180°C for 5 minutes. Fill them while still warm.

AN AROMATIC ENDING

Toward the end of this month, as long as I pick a day of suitably foul weather so that indoors is the perfect cozy retreat, I like to make my Seville orange marmalade and my mincemeat for next Christmas's mince pies at the same time. One sticky kitchen is a small price to pay for jars and jars which will feed us from January through to December. For many years I thought making my own mincemeat was too much bother, because a good store-bought one was perfectly lovely. If you feel the same way, I urge you to give homemade mincemeat a go now, when there are fewer demands on our time. Joining forces with friends, so you can share the cost and the spoils, is perhaps a more appealing starting point!

The very act of packing away the fruits of these labors is highly symbolic for me; my favorite quarter of the calendar is punctuated with a satisfyingly aromatic full stop. A gently creative January leaves me revitalized and restored, ready to tackle whatever the coming year brings. Looking back over the festive session, I sense more than ever that the benefits of spending time with loved ones, in our places of sanctuary (whether indoors or out!), are probably greater than they've ever been. So many of us have unprecedented comfort and opportunity, yet we have more isolation and separation than our forebears could have imagined.

A midwinter commemoration offers us a chance to be properly together; to pause, share, and be thankful for what and who we have in our lives. In rock bottom form, Christmas could become a box-ticking exercise of video calls on December 25th, home delivery Christmas lunches, and a present-fest of internet ordered pre-wrapped purchases. For those of us who believe in and aspire to the very antithesis of that description—a Christmas celebrated well—then taking concerted steps to appreciate, cherish, and preserve its true spirit is our privileged responsibility. Many of us may no longer regard its faithful commemoration as the means to heavenly salvation, but by making merry in a kind, inclusive, and mindful way, we might surely help our earthly one.

Long live Mrs Christmas!

BIBLIOGRAPHY

I am indebted to the marvelous resources of the Bodleian Library in Oxford and the British Library in London, where I found advice on preparing for Christmas in old books and women's magazines through the ages. Much of my own material and recipes has been gathered over the decades, filed, finessed, scribbled on, and stuck in scrapbooks. This makes detailed accreditation somewhat tricky, though my treasured stack of reference books and magazines likely hold the key.

page 13: *Wife and Home* (December 1935)
page 62: *Keeping Christmas* (SPCK, 1865)
page 67: *Good Housekeeping*, (December 1925)
page 87: *Keeping Christmas* (SPCK, 1865)
page 116: *Woman's World* (December 5th, 1925)
page 116: *Wife and Home* (December 1942)
page 122: Eliza Hackett, *The Holly Tree* (JS Crossley, 1851)

page 122: *The Christmas Tree; a Book of Instruction and Amusement* (James Blackwood, 1856)
page 126: *The Lady* (December 4th, 1969)
page 128: *The Woman's Magazine* (December 1906)
page 138: *Keeping Christmas* (SPCK, 1865)
page 138: *Good Housekeeping* (December 1944)

RESOURCES

MAGAZINES

Among my stash of cuttings sit many from the following:
Waitrose Kitchen
Waitrose Food
BBC Good Food
Country Living
Good Housekeeping
and the supremely stylish German publication *Landlust*.

BOOKS

I could not contemplate Christmas without these inspirational books to hand:
Delia Smith, *Delia Smith's Christmas* (BBC Books, 1990)
Nigel Slater, *The Christmas Chronicles* (Fourth Estate, 2017)
Nigella Lawson, *Nigella Christmas* (Chatto & Windus, 2014)
Felicity Cloake, *Completely Perfect* (Fig Tree, 2018)
Gizzi Erskine, *Gizzi's Season's Eatings* (Mitchell Beazley, 2016)
James Ramsden, *Do-Ahead Christmas* (Pavilion Books, 2014)
Meik Wiking, *The Little Book of Hygge* (Penguin Life, 2016)

Bringing resonance and meaning to our celebrations like nothing else, this is a must for all fans of the season:
Judith Flanders, *Christmas: A History* (Picador, 2017)

ONLINE

I have a few go-to websites for crafty inspiration:
pinterest.co.uk
geo.de
countryliving.com
sostrenegrene.com

Please take a peek at my own website too:
www.mrschristmasworkshop.co.uk

You can download further copies of the blank charts and planner pages in this book from the publisher's website:
www.rylandpeters.com

INDEX

ACKNOWLEDGMENTS

A mighty "thank you" to Camilla Seymour and Sheena Stockley, who set me the delightful challenge of compiling an organizational countdown to Christmas. Imagining the two of them champagne-relaxed and reclined upon their sofas next Christmas Eve truly kept me going! As did—literally—my brilliant and kind husband, Jonny, whose tolerance for my love of all things Christmassy (and drastic domestic chaos due to publishing pressures) was tested to the limit.

Inspiration for my writing flowed freely from my own childhood Christmases, always made so utterly magical for me and my sisters, Natalie, Briony, and Melanie, by our dearest Mum and Dad, Elizabeth and Ken; and from the contributions of so many "Mrs" Christmases, who so generously shared their logistics and tips with me, which I know will enrich my own festive celebrations in the years ahead.

May that be true too, for Robert Gwyn Palmer and for Cindy Richards at CICO Books, whose combined belief in my project will, I hope, help sprinkle some extra festive magic in homes far and wide! My warmest thanks for their support. Along the way, I have been heartened by many kind souls who have gone the extra mile with their time and thoughts, especially Trudi Brunskill, Beverly Hams, Heather Holden-Brown, Anna Solomon, Tim Lines, and Holly B.